CANADA'S RAINCOAST AT RISK: ART FOR AN OIL-FREE COAST

CANADA'S RAINCOAST AT RISK

Art for an Oil-Free Coast

Foreword DAVID SUZUKI Afterword WADE DAVIS

RAINCOAST CONSERVATION FOUNDATION

They call it time before memory—a time so long ago that the voices of history no longer recount an unbroken story. Some is written in the landscapes and waterways. It surfaces in myths and legends still recalled and passed down. It is carved into stone and painted on impossibly high ledges as petroglyphs and pictographs. It speaks if you stand on an open West Coast beach or deep in an ancient rainforest.

Fifty artists have come together to share their inspirations from one of the greatest wilderness treasures on Earth. Many travelled from the deep fiords to the outer rocky shores to watch grizzly bears feeding in an estuary, sea otters rolling in the kelp, or a humpback whale breaking the surface with huge breaths. Each artist has taken something from their individual experience on this collective journey to share as their expression of the story of this coast.

As the past merges into the present, we must choose our future wisely. The risk from a tar sands pipeline and oil tanker traffic is unfathomable. It is our hope that looking through this book will inspire you to join with us to stand up for an oil-free coast.

—SHERRY KIRKVOLD

CONTENTS

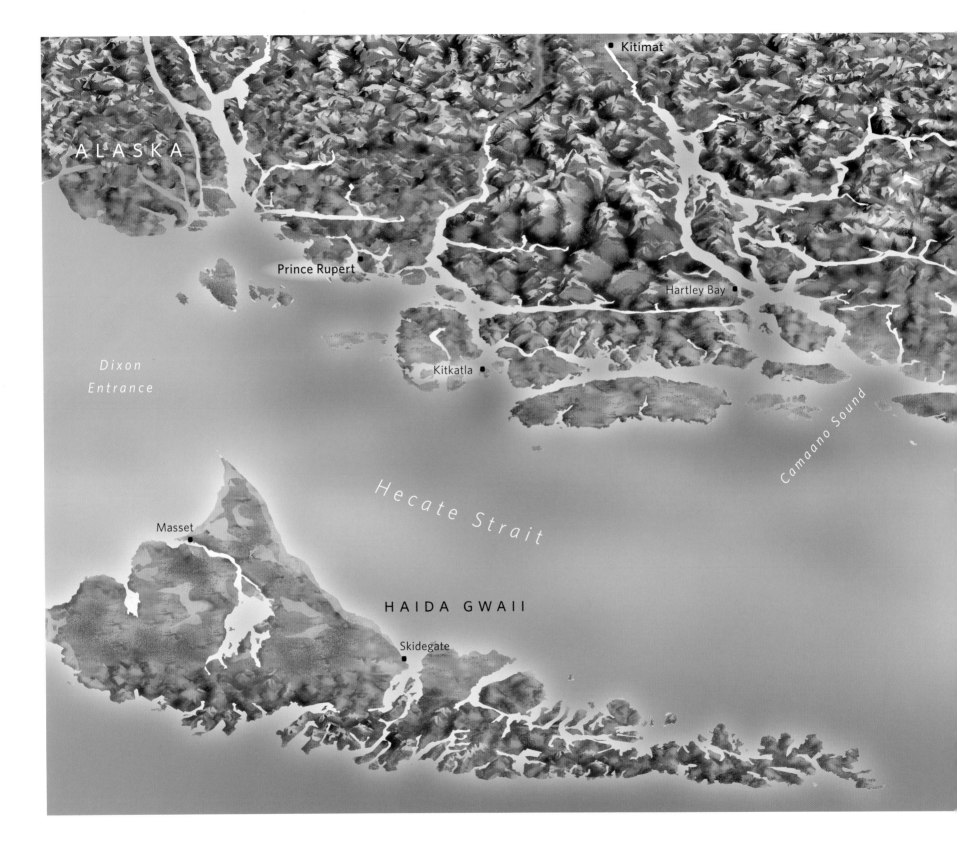

ALASKA

Kitimat

Prince Rupert

Hartley Bay

Dixon Entrance

Kitkatla

Camaano Sound

Hecate Strait

Masset

HAIDA GWAII

Skidegate

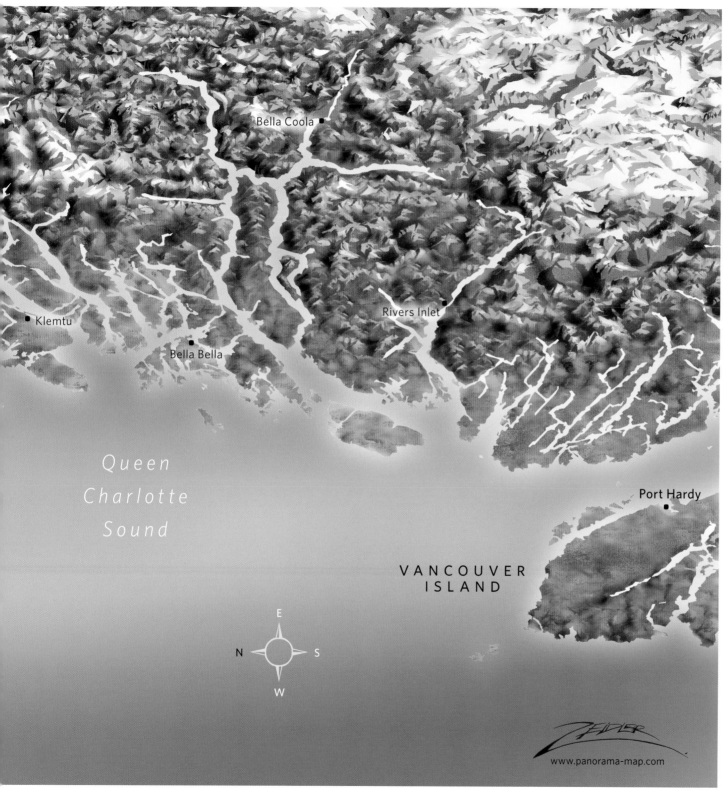

Bella Coola

Klemtu

Bella Bella

Rivers Inlet

Queen
Charlotte
Sound

VANCOUVER
ISLAND

Port Hardy

N
E
S
W

www.panorama-map.com

ALASKA

Area
of main
map

Haida
Gwaii

Kitimat

BRITISH
COLUMBIA

Vancouver
Island

Vancouver

Victoria

N
W   E
S

WASHINGTON
STATE

Canada's
Raincoast

British Columbia's
Queen Charlotte Basin

Foreword

DAVID SUZUKI

BRITISH COLUMBIA'S QUEEN CHARLOTTE BASIN is an exquisite archipelago bounded by land and ocean. It changes by the hour, the seasons, and over millennia. The region, with its thousands of islands and inlets, encompasses Haida Gwaii and the Great Bear Rainforest, all of which is nourished by the waters of the North Pacific.

The area hosts a remarkable diversity of plants and wildlife that have supported people for thousands of years. It is home to the spirit bear; some of the world's largest whales; ancient forests; magnificent runs of wild salmon; and a rich, varied, and continuing history of aboriginal culture. Enbridge's proposal to build a pipeline from the Alberta tar sands to Kitimat, BC, where the diluted bitumen (dilbit) would be loaded onto supertankers, puts it all in jeopardy. Human error, mechanical failure, unpredictable weather, and geological conditions all increase the risk of pipeline ruptures, and the loaded supertankers would face similar threats as they navigate the twisting coastal channels en route to the Pacific Ocean and Asia.

The Northern Gateway pipeline proposal has galvanized people from all walks of life and all parts of British Columbia and Canada to work toward a common goal. But that goal must be greater than just stopping the pipeline project. I have visited every First Nation community along the North and Central Coasts. With high levels of unemployment, people in those communities are desperate for jobs and economic development. Yet despite the millions of dollars in incentives offered by Enbridge, they remain unified and adamantly opposed to the pipeline. In so doing, they inform us that some things transcend money and that ecosystems that have sustained them for thousands of years are sacred and priceless.

The biosphere, our home, is under assault. We humans have grown so numerous, powerful, and demanding that we are undermining the very life support systems of the planet. That is the perspective through which opposition to the pipeline derives its energy.

Bitumen from the tar sands represents carbon energy captured from the sun and stored by nature for millions of years. To release that carbon by burning it wastefully and rapidly and to then attempt to recapture some of it and bury it again is lunacy. Science tells us that we must move quickly to renewable, clean, and limitless sources of energy long before conventional sources of energy are depleted.

In elevating the economy and the unsustainable notion of endless growth, we leave our children, grandchildren, and many generations to come with an enormous burden of ecological degradation and poverty. Unless we shift our thinking on the tar sands from the human perspective of economics and politics to the biophysical reality that we remain utterly dependent on nature for our well-being and survival, we will fail to achieve a truly rich and sustainable future.

Accelerating the unchecked exploitation of Earth's finite land, air, fresh water, and oceans—all in the name of economic growth—is unsustainable and mortgages the future by creating a massive ecological debt. Failure to reconcile ecology and economics is a hallmark of

Canadian domestic policy. Ecologists determine the conditions, principles, and laws that enable species, including us, to survive and flourish within the community of life that inhabits the zone of air, water, and land that we call the biosphere. Ecological knowledge should provide the limits and constraints of human activity.

We live in a world shaped by laws of science. From physics, we know that we cannot escape laws governing the speed of light, gravity, and entropy. Similarly, chemistry has diffusion constants, reaction rates, and atomic properties that determine the kinds of chemical reactions we can perform, the time required, and the kinds of molecules that can be synthesized. Biology shows us that as mammals, we require clean air, clean water, clean soil and food, and energy from photosynthesis for our health and well-being. Amazingly, our fundamental biological needs are provided by the web of all species that we call biodiversity. Biology dictates that these needs must be protected and nurtured above any other human activity.

Human constructs, on the other hand, can be changed. Indeed, they are the only things that we can manage, change, and adapt. We draw lines around property, cities, provinces, and nations, which we take so seriously that we kill and die to protect them. Yet nature pays no attention to human boundaries. Think of the salmon that are born in Canadian waters and travel through the Alaskan panhandle and along its coast, some migrating as far as Russia and Japan. It makes no sense to try to manage them through the priorities of our political borders.

Other human creations—capitalism, economies, corporations, markets—emerge from the human mind, not as some force of nature. The rhetoric around markets, freeing them to let them do their thing, depending on them to work things out, suggests that we regard them as seriously as we once did dragons, demons, and monsters. Yet, like dragons and demons of the past, the market is a creation of the human mind. If it doesn't adequately serve our needs and purposes, we can change it.

Fifty years after the publication of Rachel Carson's seminal book *Silent Spring,* we desperately need to consider again her urgent plea. Humanity has become so powerful in numbers, technological power, and consumptive demand that we are altering the physical, chemical, and biological properties of the planet on a geological scale, jeopardizing all species, including people. This has led Nobel Prize-winning atmospheric chemist Paul Crutzen to suggest that we are living in the Anthropocene epoch. Rachel Carson also pointed out that in the real world where wind blows, rain falls, and snow and ice appear and disappear through the seasons, everything is connected to everything else. And so when pesticides like DDT are sprayed on farmers' fields, they end up in fish, birds, and human beings.

As we learn more about the relationships of species with their environment, we come to cherish the animals, plants, waters, and lands that make us so fortunate as Canadians. This natural heritage makes up the very soul of our country and is the wealth that provides emotional and physical sustenance. The true value of our irreplaceable healthy ecosystems is priceless, immeasurable in monetary terms.

DR. DAVID SUZUKI is a scientist, broadcaster, author, and co-founder of the David Suzuki Foundation. He is professor emeritus at the University of British Columbia and holds twenty-seven honourary degrees from universities around the world. He is familiar to television audiences as host of the long-running CBC television program *The Nature of Things* and to radio audiences as the original host of CBC Radio's *Quirks and Quarks,* as well as the acclaimed series *It's a Matter of Survival* and *From Naked Ape to Superspecies.* His written work includes more than fifty-two books, nineteen of them for children.

As if a Raven

At the end of forty days Noah opened
the window of the ark which he had made,
and sent forth a raven. — Genesis 8:6–7

Something in the name Raven makes you think hot
dried   blood blackred
why would anyone trust this bird

                                        to come back
and not flap its crooked wings
in the new wild earth
making mountains where none were and monsters
it imagined   ravenravingravenous

You want to hear its call
know that something in fact *is* out there
powerful enough   a totem to the sky and rain and water
that could harness this bird and call it back
it calling you back

                your mortality

                        this being

YVONNE BLOMER

Crane's Eye View

Top: Outer shore islets | SHERRY KIRKVOLD
Centre, from left:
Flying to Hartley Bay | SHERRY KIRKVOLD
Sandhill crane | MARIE O'SHAUGHNESSY
Below: Rocky shoreline | MARK HOBSON

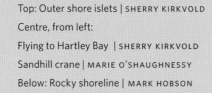

Nine million years ago, the landscape that we now call the Great Bear to Haida Gwaii would have been mostly recognizable, from a bird's-eye view. The massive mountains of the mainland, incised inlets with waterfalls and roaring creeks depositing sediment into estuaries, and scattered islands with their lacy shores of Pacific foam were all in place, even then. The grandiose architecture of the coast was created by a spectacular episode of continent building. The exotic chain of volcanic islands called Wrangellia had "docked" into the North American continental plate after a 400-million-year drift across the Pacific.

It was far from a gentle docking—more a train wreck of twisted granite—producing enough heat to create the contorted geologic forms of sheer rock faces and scattered islets. Steaming hotsprings and volcanoes were more active, but the same summer fogs and winter mists rolled in from the sea. The vegetation would also have looked similar— lush forests at sea level petering out to scrub as the slopes steepened or the exposure increased. Bald bogs dominated the uplands, protected by monastic fringes of cedar-like sequoia trees with familiar mosses, clubmosses, lichens, and ferns lining the understory, while kelp forests rimmed the shores.

13

During the moments of sunshine, we joined the cranes preening, snoozing, and rejoicing at spring.

At night, we lay in the saturated sphagnum moss, shivering and waiting for the first birds to arrive at

low tide alongside wolves, bears, and a fling of sandpipers.

14

Nine million years ago, it is also conceivable that a sandhill crane could have been flying over; the fossil remains of cranes are indistinguishable from today's cranes, making it the world's oldest living bird. This large, elegant creature matches the hues of the granite, rockweed, and peat moss so perfectly that it leaves no doubt that the bird and the place are intertwined. Even then, the cranes may well have migrated to remote island nesting sites to escape the ancestors of our modern-day wolves. Familiar whales would have been feeding around the shores, seals and sea lions lounging on rocks, and otters diving in the kelp beds. The water was starting to cool as the great glacial cycles of the Pleistocene began.

For the last three million years, sheets of ice pulsed in and out and sea levels rose up and down, never fully wiping the granite clean. Refugia persisted at the edges, especially where the ice hit the sea and the upwelling nutrients supported marine life—cranes among them. It has always been a highly productive ecosystem at the edge, where currents, clouds, and continents collide; where fresh and salt water mingle; and where geography creates endless niches for life to flourish.

The human relationship to the land is relatively short compared to that of the cranes. I learned this from Jessie Housty and her people. Jessie was my research assistant, though trained as a poet. She is also the granddaughter of a Heiltsuk chief in whose vast territory we were researching the *c'idawai*, the coastal Canadian sandhill crane—*Grus canadensis rowani*—described as such by the western scientists because it "disappeared" to Canada to breed. Protected by remoteness

and weather, this subspecies not only bypassed predators but also western science—a huge achievement in itself. Where they breed precisely was known only by Jessie's people—unacceptable data, it appears, when it comes to judicial reviews of oil tanker impacts.

We were surveying 300 kilometres from Vancouver, as the crane flies, in the heart of their breeding range: the tiny islets in pools within bogs on islands in the vast archipelago surrounded by the moody Pacific that oil tankers are proposing to navigate through. Our boat was a solid aluminum herring punt with a big fossil fuel-fired engine to cover the huge distances and cope with terrible sea conditions—the paradox was not lost on the poet.

Jessie and I moved through the territory taking up different vantage points to watch cranes, from makeshift blinds in the inland lagoons where the non-breeding cranes gather to practise their courtship dances, to remote islets where the pairs bond and establish their nests up in the bogs. During the moments of sunshine, we joined the cranes preening, snoozing, and rejoicing at spring. At night, we lay in the saturated sphagnum moss, shivering and waiting for the first birds to arrive at low tide alongside wolves, bears, and a fling of sandpipers.

The collective noun for cranes is a "siege of cranes," and that is what it feels like when they darken a dawn sky already dimmed with mist, calling in their haunting, prehistoric language. They fly in formation, long necks and legs outstretched as they spiral down to a slow-motion landing. We were out to collect data on these birds, but Jessie also writes poems about their beauty. In the battle over BC's coast, it is not

Forest waterfall | SHERRY KIRKVOLD

clear whether poetry or data will be the most powerful weapon. We collected both.

We were part of a larger team of scientists and traditional knowledge holders documenting the range of species on the coast to improve their chances against industrial interests. The cranes' existence has no doubt been challenged many times over the last nine million years—most recently at the turn of the twentieth century by overhunting in their southern winter range—but they were making a comeback. The one western scientific documentation was made by Dr. McTaggart-Cowan in 1939. He recorded a pair feeding in a lagoon on Spider Island and recommended we return—more than sixty years later—as he suspected they were faithful to good nesting sites. Spider Island is an impenetrable navigational nightmare but is a highly productive dream site for breeding cranes. We set up a blind in the lagoon, then waited. Suddenly a pair of cranes arrived on a poetic nuptial flight path that was conceivably nine million years old.

Each researcher in this book has a similar story, involving a flock, a pod, a pack, a school, a fling, or a siege of a particular species as well as the mountain, forest, estuary, or shoreline that they inhabit, interact with, and move seasonally through. Read as a collective, these stories begin to paint a picture of this ancient landscape. The researchers collect data, but as you can see through their collaboration with artists and poets, the greater power is in the ability to connect us all both mind and heart to this incredible refugia at the edge of the world.

BRIONY PENN's roots on the coast go back five generations. She is a geographer by training; a writer, artist, and naturalist by trade; and an educator and activist by vocation. She's been a journalist for print and TV and an adjunct professor/lecturer at the University of Victoria. She works every spring on the coast as a naturalist and is currently writing the biography of scientist/activist Ian McTaggart-Cowan.

15

ROBERT BATEMAN

MARK HOBSON

"I can't conceive of anything being more varied, rich, and handsome than planet Earth; its crowning beauty is the natural world. I want to soak it up, to understand it . . . then put it together and express it in my painting. This is the way I want to dedicate my life."

Robert Bateman's realistic painting style, featuring wildlife in its habitat, encourages the viewer to examine the natural world and reflects his commitment to ecology. Besides being one of Canada's best-known artists, he is a spokesperson for many environmental issues. The subject of numerous books and films, his honours and awards are many, including twelve honourary doctorates, three schools named after him, and Officer of the Order of Canada. His artistic legacy will soon be displayed at the new Bateman Centre in Victoria, BC, with educational initiatives through both the Centre and Royal Roads University.

>
Calvert Island Eagle
Oil on canvas
61 x 91 cm

Palette for plein air colour studies

MIKE SVOB

MARK HOBSON

Mike Svob is celebrating his thirtieth year as a professional artist. He is an impressionist easily identified by his signature use of strong, bold colour. Fluent in watercolours, acrylics, and oils, Mike has had more than seventy exhibitions and produced twenty-five-plus murals throughout North America. He enjoys the creative process and is an avid map reader and a pilot—a person with a great sense of adventure. His passion for travel and history has led him to a diverse range of subject matter.

Svob's paintings are held in many private and corporate collections throughout the world. His work has been featured in *International Artists Magazine, Magazin'Art, Artist Magazine,* and *American Artist.* His paintings and ideas about painting can be found in several art books. He studied at the University of Western Ontario and is a past president and senior member of the Federation of Canadian Artists.

>
Calvert Island Beach
Acrylic on canvas
61 x 91 cm

Hakai beach

DOMINIK J. MODLINSKI

Dominik J. Modlinski was born in Warsaw, Poland, in 1970. He studied fine arts at Ontario College of Art in Toronto, where he graduated with honours in 1993. In the early '90s his travels led him to the Yukon wilderness and the far North, where he truly found his inner creative calling: depicting the dramatic landscapes of Canada.

Dominik's painting journeys are a wilderness experience based upon weeks of travelling rugged and barren lands to capture, in plein air style, the majesty of nature. His northern travels have inspired him to explore further and visit many of Earth's last remaining wilderness areas. Some of his most extreme painting expeditions have taken him across continents and hemispheres such as Antarctica, the High Arctic, Greenland, Patagonia, and most recently into the wilds of Namibia and South Africa.

>
*In the Land of
the Spirit Bear*
Oil on board
51 x 76 cm

PAUL JORGENSEN

SHERRY KIRKVOLD

Paul Jorgensen was born in Tofino in 1947 and at an early age moved to Nanaimo, BC, where he now lives and works from his home studio. Paul's passion for art started early—painting has always been a part of his life—and for the last twelve years it has been his full-time endeavour. Encouraged by his teachers and parents, he graduated from the Vancouver School of Art (now known as Emily Carr University of Art + Design) and for a short time worked in graphic design. Paul's journey into traditional and academic painting gave way to a more imagined landscape. Saturated in rich colours, Paul's work is influenced by the Impressionists and the Group of Seven.

Paul's recent trip to the untouched natural landscape of the Great Bear Rainforest has deeply concerned him with questions of human sustainability in such a delicate and pristine ecosystem.

>
Reflecting on an Endless Coastline
Acrylic on canvas
91 x 91 cm

It really struck me that each of the creatures in and around the sea, every single life form, is entirely dependent upon the quality of the water. When given the choice of a myriad wonderful subjects, I chose to paint this remote beach on Banks Island because of its pristine, crystal clear water.

CAROL EVANS

BRYN KING

Carol Evans was born in Vancouver and currently lives with her husband on Salt Spring Island, British Columbia. Evans is a self-taught artist, developing skills with watercolours over a period of thirty years. She has had seventeen one-woman shows and participated in many group exhibitions. Her paintings reflect a reverent attitude towards the beauty of the British Columbia shoreline, as if to hold it up and say, "Look at this! Isn't it magnificent, isn't it exquisite, and aren't we fortunate to have this ocean so full of life?" always in the hope that if we appreciate and love something, we'll look after it. Her paintings have been published in the books *West Coast: Homeland of Mist*; *Releasing the Light*; and *The Shores We Call Home*. Evans' work has achieved international acclaim and is represented in exhibitions and private collections worldwide.

>
Banks Island
Watercolour
91 x 122 cm

From the highlands of the Rockies and the glaciers of BC, our fresh waters wend their way in ever increasing volume down to our coastal inlet estuaries to disperse in ocean salt water. The access to deepwater ports is treacherously convoluted, with strong and erratic tidal flows, submerged rocks, reefs, steep cliffs, and unpredictable wind forces.

My painting, Northern Gateway, *depicts a frontal overview of the portals of the BC continental coastline, simplified as granite and water sculpture.*

STEWART MARSHALL

GAYE ADAMS

Stewart grew up in Montreal, where he also received his art education. Intrigued by First Nations art, he travelled to the West Coast and built his first kayak to transport himself and his art supplies north. For forty years he has left in early spring and returned in late fall with the many paintings and sketches created while travelling alone, camping, painting, and living off the land and sea.

Stewart has experienced many difficulties and life-threatening events on the coast, but he never feared. However, the ominous likelihood of an eventual oil spill on our coast causes him to fear. He feels a debt of gratitude to all those who have treated him so kindly on this fine coastline, plus a commitment to help preserve the lives of all those beings that can do nothing to protect themselves.

\>
Northern Gateway
Watercolour
37 x 46 cm

ROBERTA SUTHERLAND

LORNE BROWNSEY

Roberta was born and raised on BC's West Coast never far from a shore-line. She attended Emily Carr College of Art + Design and received a BFA from the University of Victoria. Her varied experiences have included working with CUSO in East Africa, training in print making in the UK, and studying Zen and calligraphy in Japan. She has had painting residencies at Banff Centre and Bau Insitute in Italy. She has also served as a mentor for the Metchosin International Summer School of the Arts. Roberta's work has been collected by the Canada Council and public galleries. In 2012 she was the Geneva Editart "Cercle des Amis" artist. For inspiration she is grateful to Jack Wise and the Northwest School. She has a lifelong fascination with the patterns of nature and how they repeat themselves in all of creation. Her main studio is at Grassy Point, Hornby Island, BC.

>
Homage to G.S.
Watercolour
40 x 50 cm

Oxsuli Remembered

The elder offered to show me a place where the *oxsuli** were just starting to grow back. A shift in the river had wiped out the mud flats that *oxsuli* prefer. We took a speedboat out to the site and I tied up on shore. *Oxsuli* grow tall in heart-shaped elliptic leaves. The tiny greenish-yellow flowers droop from the top in tassels. The berries are highly toxic and range from beige to deep red. The *oxsuli* we found were only knee-high. As she touched a leaf, she told me a story about her grandmother teaching her about *oxsuli* just as she was teaching me. She bent over further and cleared away some dirt, exposing the root, a stringy orange cluster. I knew the root was used to keep ghosts away and for good luck, but she told me how to use the root to cure headaches.

"You should get to know its energy," she said. "Lean in and study it."

"Okay."

"I'm glad they're growing back here," she said. "They haven't for a long time."

As I leaned in to study the *oxsuli,* my rubber boots slipped in the mud and I fell on top of it and squashed it.

The elder was quiet as I picked myself up and tried to unsquash the plant.

"Maybe you should stick to writing," she said.

EDEN ROBINSON

*The English name for *oxsuli* is false hellebore.

JESSIE HOUSTY

A Legacy of Culture and Stewardship

Top: Jessie Housty and
nephew Landon | CHRIS DARIMONT
Centre, from left:
Uncompleted canoe | SHERRY KIRKVOLD
Mortuary pole | BEN FOX
Interior of Klemtu Big House
| KAJ R. SVENSSON
Below: Chester Starr (Lone Wolf)
| CHRIS DARIMONT

As First Nations on British Columbia's North and Central Coast, we have been intimately tied to our traditional lands and waters since time before memory. Each Nation has its own creation story, but each one winds in the same direction: when the Creator put our peoples here, we were born into a symbiotic interdependence. We are still peoples who cannot be separated from our lands and waters. Our identity is still rooted in our traditional territories and written on the landscape in the lines of stories that have been passed down generation to generation for more than ten thousand years.

The Great Bear Rainforest is a large region, spanning roughly 70,000 kilometres of wilderness and bright water. Broken down, it encompasses the territories of nearly thirty First Nations and, within each Nation, the lands of many tribes, families, and hereditary chiefs. Every pictograph and petroglyph, every stone fishtrap and trapline, every canoe blank and culturally modified tree is another inhale or exhale in the storytelling of the coast. Every interaction between our peoples and the lands and waters of our home harkens back to a time when we could transform into other beings, live in the landscape in other ways.

31

Our reliance on our homeland's bounty is not simply about taking what we need to sustain ourselves. It is about a debt to the lands and waters that have nurtured our peoples since time immemorial—and about a promise to future generations that we will hand down the same bounty to them and their children.

The pattern of abandoned village sites across our territories maps our retreat to places of strength in the wake of smallpox and influenza, residential schools, and other injuries to our wellness as First Nations peoples that decimated our populations and brought us to the brink of extinguishment. From those central places of strength—modern townsites such as Hartley Bay, Klemtu, Bella Bella, Kitamaat Village, Rivers Inlet, Old Massett, and Skidegate—where our remaining peoples came together, we are beginning to spread ourselves out again across a landscape that has waited for us through broken generations. Our story as a people is punctuated by threats, but the narrative thread of survival and resurgence is just as clear.

In every facet of our traditional way of life, biodiversity and cultural diversity are inextricably linked. Our clan system identifies us with the bear, raven, eagle, wolf, and with many others—brothers and sisters who share our territories and their stories with us. The crests we wear as families and individuals represent names, genealogies, and narratives as much about the landscape as the peoples who inhabit it. Our responsibility to all that surrounds us is a rich duty born of a culture that brings our lands and waters and all they contain into a sacred unity within us. They are facets of ourselves, and we are a part of them.

Today, we are building on our traditional values and place-based identity to carry us into a future of community wellness and cultural resilience that looks very different from the world our ancestors lived in. We share our homelands with people whose part in the coast's long narrative is a choice: fishermen, the descendants of cannery workers—people to whom the lands and waters speak, drawing them into the story. We face threats unimagined even just a few generations ago. The rich, wild bounty of the coast attracts the gaze of people who do not hear it speak, who simply see price tags and possibilities. More than an antagonist, tar sands crude shipped through these waters threatens an abrupt end to the deep stories of the coast.

Today, a coast that once seemed remote to those beyond its dense forests and untamed waters is suddenly at the centre of debates on the global stage. For our ancestors, and for the promise of future generations and the next ten thousand years to come, coastal First Nations are standing up as guardians and warriors. We are learning to blend the traditional and the modern to find strength in the middle ground. We are linking sound science with traditional ecological knowledge to lay a foundation for decision making around our traditional territories and resources. We are forging alliances based on deep values and a vision for a wild coast.

We still live in a place where we can walk through the forest and see the fallen, mossy beams of big houses where our grandmothers were born. We can nourish our children with salmon and halibut from our grandfathers' fishing grounds, with deer and mountain goat from the places our grandfathers' grandfathers hunted. We can do this because our stories' power invests us as stewards of our homelands. Our ancestors anticipated us. Hundreds and thousands of years ago, without knowing our names or the way we would live, their values taught

them to remember we were coming and to live in a balance we would someday learn to emulate ourselves. Future generations will look at the decisions we make now in the same way we look to our ancestors for strength and guidance that echo from the First Generation of our creation stories.

Our reliance on our homeland's bounty is not simply about taking what we need to sustain ourselves. It is about a debt to the lands and waters that have nurtured our peoples since time immemorial—and about a promise to future generations that we will hand down the same bounty to them and their children. We are part of a gift economy with nature and the future, and we mimic it in the potlatch system that upholds the wealthiest people—the ones who give the most away—as indisputably powerful leaders.

Every culture evolves. We do not, as First Nations peoples, live the way our ancestors did one or ten or a hundred generations ago. Neither does the landscape look exactly the same as it did thousands of years past. But there is something irrefutable at the core of our cultural identity that remains unchanged through time, and as we have adapted to our changing lands and waters, we have aligned ourselves to the rhythm of the coast.

Sea-bright salmon return to their natal streams through all the hazards of the coastal waters. Migratory birds, brushstrokes against the sky, draw powerful lines between the beginnings and ends of their journeys. Wherever we go in the world, we are people of the Great Bear Rainforest. These lands and waters speak to us and through us, and

their stories have a richness and strength that nourish and sustain us. We derive our authority from our relationship to place, and our identity is rooted in a coast that bears witness to our entire history as First Nations peoples.

In turn, we simply ask that you join us, as allies and warriors and storytellers in your own right, in bearing similar witness to the coast whose own story risks erasure. Together, we will ensure that future generations tell the story of this moment as a narrative of resilience and power—the triumph of gentle warriors in the name of deeply wild places.

JESSIE HOUSTY is a member of the Heiltsuk First Nation in Bella Bella, British Columbia. She is a director at Qqs Projects Society, a community-driven non-profit organization building cultural and natural stewardship capacity in the Great Bear Rainforest. She is pursuing her MA in English at the University of Victoria.

33

Bear Mask

SHAWN ASTER

Shawn was born in Vancouver, BC, in 1980 and raised by his grandfather in his late mother's community of Gitkxaala (Kitkatla), a small Tsimshian community southwest of Prince Rupert on the north side of Dolphin Island (Lach klan). The name Kitkatla derives from the Tsimshian name Gitkxaała, from git- (people of) and kxaała (open sea), since they are the farthest from the mainland of the Tsimshian Nations.

Shawn comes from the Ganhada (Raven) Clan, House of Dzewalaks. He was inspired to create art at an early age by seeing the remaining totem poles in his community and by his environment. Shawn also became aware of his late mother's interest in Northwest Coast art, and this fueled his passion. He always wants to improve and learn more about his culture.

"I get a fulfilling sense of pride portraying my culture through the classic Northwest Coast art."

>
*Bentwood Chest
End Design*
Redcedar, acrylic,
abalone sheet
56 x 71 cm

This mask represents the ancestors, as we all descend from a human family. The blue refers to the ocean; it is important to keep our coast pure so we can continue to live off the ocean. This brings us to the land, for the land and the ocean are so tightly woven together that they are, in a sense, one being. We cannot separate the land from the water or stop the sacred cycle of the water going from the glaciers to the rivers, to the ocean, back up to clouds, and then falling back to the mountains where it began.

IAN REID

BEN FOX

Ian Reid is a Heiltsuk artist and cultural leader, born in 1978 in Bella Bella, BC. His ancestral name is Nusi (Full Moon). Ian's art is inspired by the cultural knowledge of Heiltsuk elders and enriched by his research into Heiltsuk and Northwest Coast art in museums in Europe and the USA. His mentors include the late Heiltsuk artist David Gladstone, the late Cyril Carpenter, and Kwakwaka'wakw artist Simon Dick.

Ian's work has been featured in numerous galleries and exhibits. It includes portrait and transformation masks, totem poles, panels, an 11-metre cedar canoe, as well as mixed media, bentwood boxes, acrylics, and ceremonial regalia. Ian is currently working on four house poles for the Big House in Bella Bella.

Ian is a mentor and inspiration to young Heiltsuk and urban Aboriginal artists through his commitment to the continuing relevance and vitality of Heiltsuk art.

>
Ancestor Mask
Redcedar, paint, horse hair, rope
20 x 14 x 14 cm

Visions of the Future, Visions of the Past. Elected Chief Doug Neasloss

DAVID GOATLEY

KAJ R. SVENSSON

David Goatley is widely recognized as one of North America's leading portrait painters. Born in London, England, he trained at the Camberwell School of Art and began painting full time in 1990, following a successful career in advertising. He came to North America in 1992, settling his family in Victoria, BC, and travelling to fulfill commissions across Canada, the United States, and England—around three hundred in the past twenty years. His portraits have included a prime minister, speaker, and premier; three lieutenant governors; leaders in academia, business, law, medicine, and the arts; as well as many individuals and families.

Exhibitions include the retrospective *A Shared Journey: The Portraits of David Goatley* at the Nanaimo Art Gallery, as well as solo and group shows that tell visual stories about the people and places visited on his travels both here and in Europe, India, and the Middle East.

>
Telling It Like It Is
Chief Charlie Mason,
Kitsasoo/Xai'xais
First Nation
Oil on canvas
92 x 76 cm

Chief Charlie Mason

MICHAEL O'TOOLE

KAJ R. SVENSSON

Michael was born in 1963 in Vancouver, BC, and grew up in West Vancouver. He studied architectural design at BCIT and worked doing pre-
sentational renderings in Toronto. Back in Vancouver, he became a full-
time fine artist in 1992. Michael received signature status through the
Federation of Canadian Artists in 2000. He is represented in several galleries across Canada and his work is in countless corporate and private
collections around the world. He has been featured in *International Artists*
and *Magazin'Art*. He has given workshops to artist guilds across Canada
and the USA.

Michael paints mostly in acrylic, but also works in watercolour, oil,
graphite, and pen and ink. His subjects include landscapes, portraits,
marine, architecture, and wildlife. He is currently devoting his time and
awareness to the preservation and continuity of the Klemtu people,
marine life, and all other creatures (great and small) sheltered under the
Great Spirit Bear Rainforest.

>
*The Golden Hour
in Haida Gwaii*
Acrylic on canvas
76 x 76 cm

Halibut Catcher #1

HAROLD ALLANSON

KAJ R. SVENSSON

Harold Allanson holds a life-long interest in drawing and painting but didn't express his talent fully until he took early retirement. He then delved seriously into his art and hasn't looked back.

Much of Harold's stimulation comes from the area where he lives: the inspiring scenery of British Columbia's West Coast. Like many artists, he is acutely aware of the natural beauty around him and has an eye for shapes, patterns, and the effects of lights and darks. His watercolours depict boats and the people connected to them—the aged, battered tugs that still provide sustenance for skipper and crew, and the older fishing boats that are quickly disappearing. His paintings are bold, realistic works often expressed in strong colours, revealing water reflections late in the day, early morning sunlight, or deep shadows—the style of painting that will catch the viewer's eye from a distance.

>
Halibut Catcher #2
Watercolour
61 x 81 cm

Wolf

想看一只狼
疑是雪皮梦
鼻到尾快闪
真假都一样
反而贴在桑
原来本身声
如此人无家
盲流无祖宗

Xiǎng kàn yī zhī lǎng

Yí shì xuě pí mèng

Bí dào wěi kuài shǎn

Zhēn jiǎ dōu yī yàng

Fǎn ér tiē zài sǎng

Yuán lái běn shēn shēng

Rú cǐ rén wú jiā

Máng liú wú zū zong

Thought I saw a wolf,

Perhaps a snow-skin dream;

Nose-tail flashed real-false

Both the same it seemed.

But it stuck in my throat

My voice's predecessor,

A floating labourer,

With neither home nor ancestor.

STEVE NOYES

CHRIS DARIMONT

(Not So) Terrestrial Mammals

Top: American mink | TIM IRWIN

Centre, left to right: Wolves | KLAUS POMMERENKE

Grizzly | ERIC SAMBOL

Below: Spirit bear with salmon | SHERRY KIRKVOLD

A whiff of wolf *threw the dozing seal into full panic, sending him pinballing awkwardly down the barnacled rocks and into the safety of his watery world. Although her trespass on his small rocky refuge was detected, this top predator had found meals there before that more than compensated for the 200-metre swim. Today, however, the mother wolf needs to make up precious calories lost in the water.*

After powerful strokes propel her back to her outer coastal island, her paws strike land. Only a quick shake reveals a transition from ocean to earth before she trots, nose down, along the shoreline.

Rufous coat against intertidal algae provides little visual clue to a nervous river otter moving from the forest to the shore. A stiff southeaster at the wolf's back grants the otter enough warning, however, to risk a stubby-legged undulating dash to the sea. The wolf does not give chase, confident that her nose will lead to an even bigger prize.

The wealth of salmon have come and gone for another year here, requiring the wolf and her family to roam more widely for a meal. Before long she reunites with her two young of the year. On a rocky headland, she finds the toddlers corn-cobbing mussels off a waterlogged hemlock trunk. Between each scraping mouthful, their pink tongues transfer stray morsels from muzzle to chops. This will tide them over until the next low water.

They don't know it yet, but the ocean will bestow something very special upon them tomorrow. A beached humpback whale, stricken by old age, will donate his largesse to this family and indeed the whole island. Wolves will feast on seafood for several months, sharing the wealth with other furred and feathered fauna.

45

This geographical shoreline configuration—home to salmon streams, wolf pups, and everything in between—places this marine-terrestrial web in great peril in today's world. Spilled oil has a tendency to settle on shorelines and beaches.

This vignette could represent a typical day in the life of our atypical coastal wolf. In fact, when we speak of "wolves of the sea" here, two possibilities emerge: killer whales and grey wolves. Our First Nations friends on the coast have known for millennia that wolves here are part of the marine sphere.

Raincoast's body of scientific work—spanning more than a decade—has complemented this knowledge with some new insight and numbers. For example, chemical tracers examined in the hair wolves leave behind tell us that island wolves—like our family above—can make 50 to 75 percent of their living from seafood. Even family groups on the mainland largely forgo their staple of deer during autumn. When such a safe, nutritious, and predictable meal like salmon comes to them, who would want to behave like any old wolf?

Other so-called terrestrial animals are similarly charmed by salmon. Every member of the weasel family—from the little ermine that adorns the regalia of chiefs to the powerful wolverine—dines on salmon. In nearby Alaska, researchers have discovered that mink modify their reproduction in areas where salmon are plentiful, timing this bounty to the most energetically demanding part of motherhood: breastfeeding. We also know that the few cougars, or mountain lions, that slink through the dense rainforest surely eat salmon, but the precise relationship is still a mystery.

There is little unknown, however, about what salmon mean to bears. When salmon are scarce, so is reproduction, which demands so much energy. Therefore, when salmon are plentiful, mothers have more cubs and populations exist at higher densities. Salmon is the currency of abundance for bears on this coast.

This silvery gold seems to have bought a white coat for a black bear. Dr. Tom Reimchen, friend of Raincoast and professor at the University of Victoria, has added new insight into this extraordinary bear, sometimes called spirit or Kermode bear. While surely first appearing as a mutation, or random genetic mix-up, the white colour should have gone extinct, unless it brought some value to bears in the area. Tom's student, Dan Klinka, found that white bears have a slightly higher fishing success than their black brethren because they appear less threatening to salmon against the region's typically overcast background. So it seems that salmon gifted this terrestrial animal with a look found nowhere else.

Although salmon are the flagship animals linking the ocean to terrestrial mammals, they offer only one of many possible foundations for such relationships. New research from Raincoast's Caroline Fox is showing how herring eggs fuel intertidal invertebrate species such as sand fleas, on which black bears gorge during the spring. In a similar relationship, the black bears of Haida Gwaii—which are the largest in the world—chow down on the hard-shelled animals of the intertidal zone. River otters can live almost exclusively off intertidal and nearshore fishes and invertebrates. Marine carrion also feeds the many mammals that are renowned scavengers.

Why are these relationships between terrestrial animals and the marine environment so pronounced on BC's coast? A big reason is

Cougar | CHARLES BRANDT

geographical. BC's modest 900-kilometre north-to-south distance between Washington and Alaska contains an astonishing 27,000 kilometres of coastline that jogs around hundreds of islands and dozens of inlets. This is clearly a lot of waterfront. Far from forming a boundary between land and sea, it is on these shores where a great mixing occurs. Molecules and energy swap—from leaves flowing down rivers and into the ocean to mussel particles finding their way into the mouths of wolf pups. As if on some giant conveyor belt, adult salmon return to their natal streams to spawn and die—pumping in nutrients for a whole coastal ecosystem. Sea and land interconnect in constant exchange.

This geographical shoreline configuration—home to salmon streams, wolf pups, and everything in between—places this marine-terrestrial web in great peril in today's world. Spilled oil has a tendency to settle on shorelines and beaches. The seafood buffets with which these remarkable creatures evolved could be spoiled for many decades. Precious spawning habitat for pink and chum salmon, which choose the lower intertidal reaches of streams to breed, would be certain casualties.

Let us not forget another land-based mammal with a lot at stake. As Jessie Housty so eloquently points out, her people—and all those along this coast—are people of the ocean. If we lose this battle and accept the gamble that a pipeline and tankers impose, we risk not only wildlife but also a piece of who we are.

CHRIS DARIMONT aims to practice acutely applied and socially relevant conservation science to serve the environment and people of the Great Bear Rainforest. The GBR has been his part-time home, classroom, playground, and place of worship since the late 1990s. Chris directs science for Raincoast and is the newly appointed Hakai-Raincoast conservation scholar and assistant professor in the Department of Geography at the University of Victoria.

A single piece of Brazilian soapstone weighing 227 kilograms was carved 360 degrees over a period of fifteen months. *Raincoast Bowl* was cast from this carving and represents our coastal estuaries with wolves; black and grizzly bears; and pink, coho, and spring salmon.

CRAIG BENSON

Craig was born in Vancouver and has lived and worked his entire adult life on the British Columbia coast. His formal education includes environmental studies, wildlife management, and habitat protection.

A self-taught master carver of stone and wood, Craig began sculpting full time in 1990 and also creates original bronzes. His works are always carved from a single piece of material and almost exclusively represent local marine species in fine, realistic detail. Collectors both corporate and private throughout the world exclaim: "I feel so connected to the spirit of this creature." For some it is their first exquisite, up-close experience of a species they've either never seen before or, in some cases, were indifferent to.

Craig is unable to express the pain he feels at the thought of these creatures being annihilated and is committed to stopping the passage of oil tankers on our coast.

>
Raincoast Bowl
Bronze
76 x 97 x 28 cm

My piece combines both sea and land animals. The main form represents the salmon with the tail of a whale, and the two faces are the bear mother and cub—all of which we saw on our artists' trip.

Preparatory sketch

BEN DAVIDSON

BEN FOX

Ben is a Haida artist who draws upon his knowledge of traditional Haida design to create innovative and unique contemporary pieces that are sought after by discerning collectors around the world. He specializes in wood but also creates two-dimensional designs. Recently, he has expanded his repertoire to include jewellery and engraving. His work has been included in various multi-artist shows and is currently on display at his gallery, All About U Arts, in Haida Gwaii. His chief's seat was exhibited in the show *Raven Travelling: Two Centuries of Haida Art* and featured in the accompanying book of the same name.

Ben's dedication to the revival of Haida culture moves beyond the realm of art, as he is one of the original members of Rainbow Creek Dancers, a traditional Haida dance group. In all his work, Ben continually explores the symbiotic relationship between the ceremonial and contemporary roles of Haida art.

>
Can U Bear to See It?
Yellow-cedar
61 x 48 cm

The coastal forest is home to thousands of animals and plants, including some, like wolves,

that need large wilderness areas to survive. This forest is also a huge carbon reserve that provides

us with oxygen, but it is being destroyed by industrial activities and human encroachment.

Pipelines are just one example of industrial activity that opens up the wilderness to other

human activity. Protection of the remaining intact forest is essential not only to coastal plants

and animals but to our survival and to slow the effects of climate change.

I hope my art can help bring awareness to the importance of conserving our pristine

Canadian wilderness.

JULIA HARGREAVES

SHERRY KIRKVOLD

Chosen twice for the Leigh Yawkey Woodson *Birds in Art* exhibition and two-time Ducks Unlimited National Art Portfolio winner, internationally published BC wildlife artist Julia Hargreaves trained in England and received an MA from Manchester Metropolitan University. As a member of Artists for Conservation, her work has appeared in several of their annual exhibitions, including the inaugural exhibition at Hiram Blauvelt Art Museum, New York, and in 2008 she illustrated *Birdscapes: A Pop-Up Celebration of Bird Song.*

In 2011 she took part in a canoe trip with the Wilderness River Expedition Artists Federation to Caribou Woodland Park in Ontario to sketch and record the boreal forest as part of a project to help preserve the largest remaining intact forest on the planet. Julia is represented by Tutt St. Gallery and Picture Perfect, Kelowna; Lloyd Gallery, Penticton; Avenida Galleries, Calgary; and Robert Paul Galleries, Stowe, Vermont, USA.

>
*Wolves on the
Clean Sand*
Acrylic on board
30 x 41 cm

JEFFREY GORDON WHITING

KAJ R. SVENSSON

An award-winning sculptor, author, impresario, and environmental advocate with a background in biology and geology, Jeff is president and founder of Artists for Conservation (AFC), the world's leading artist group supporting the environment. When Jeff was sixteen, Prime Minister Brian Mulroney presented one of Jeff's sculptures to Prince Philip, and at eighteen, Jeff completed his first book and won first prize at the World Championships for Wildfowl Carving. A signature member of the Society of Animal Artists, a fellow of the Explorers Club, a Leigh Yawkey *Birds in Art* exhibitor, and recipient of Business in Vancouver's Forty Under 40 Award, Jeff has advised for Science Art-Nature at Stanford and the Robert Bateman Centre for Art and Environmental Education. He is producing a series of AFC documentary films and leading the AFC Festival—a ten-day international art and environmental education event at North Vancouver's Grouse Mountain Resort.

>
Great Bear Awakening
Bronze
22 x 33 x 20 cm

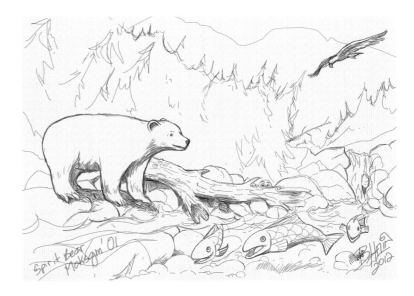

BILL HELIN

SUE MELTO HELIN

William Herbert Helin spent his pre-teen years in the northern part of the wet coast commercial fishing with his father, Arthur (Hyemass) Helin, until 1979, when a serious accident redirected him into his Native art career.

Bill studied at the famous 'Ksan Indian Art School of BC where he learned traditional design, tool making, wood carving, and jewellery engraving under Tsimshian master artists. In 1987 he studied at the Gemological Institute of America where he learned gemology and gem setting to enhance his story bracelets and wedding rings.

Bill's clients come from around the globe, and his jewellery has travelled into space on the Shuttle Columbia STS-78 in 1994. Bill has created patch designs for NASA and Canadian-born astronaut Bob Thirsk and will be creating another this year. Other passions include acrylic painting, storybook writing, illustration, sharing his Tsimshian heritage stories and songs, and teaching children the importance of their culture.

>
Eeny, Meeny, Miny…
Acrylic on board
60 x 79 cm

Fin-de-siècle Renaissance

Spencer   Hudson   fresh

water   dam   fish

cannery   rows

A little ornery
one afternoon
my mother:
      "No way
          you wanna
      know
         what they can…"

          Dead. Trees. Now
Ecological Park

       We cross the board walk. Water

       bottle. Sole muck. Think I hear

       my heart. *Gwa'wina*. A pair of

       ravens their rhythmic flap of

       wing startles the witches' hair

       moss. An

          obligatory

              raucous

croak

   followed by

      rather dramatic

          mimesis

     in reflection

   maybe

something

heard
   on a passing
       speaker
         another
           bird
             then…

Swamp   Cedars   Silence

GARRY THOMAS MORSE

PAUL PAQUET
ANITA ROCAMORA

Lush, Living Tapestries

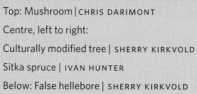

Top: Mushroom | CHRIS DARIMONT
Centre, left to right:
Culturally modified tree | SHERRY KIRKVOLD
Sitka spruce | IVAN HUNTER
Below: False hellebore | SHERRY KIRKVOLD

A walk in the forest *Giant, centuries-old trees with root crowns as big as subterranean caverns, tangled under-brush, unexpected sunlit clearings, matted layers of humus, beds of moss deep enough to swallow a man's arm, splattering waterfalls—not a space devoid of life anywhere. Impenetrable thickets of devil's club, salal, tunnels of ferns make walking off-trail difficult. Fallen, moss-covered logs span ravines. In a clearing: 2-metre-tall hellebores, mysterious pools of inky water brewed between tree roots. Trails are patiently carved along the gentlest, most energy-efficient contours of the land by a thousand generations of padded feet, and sometimes stream-beds are the only path. Being wet here is normal and both of no account and of very great importance. Very few days are with-out rain or mist or rivers to cross. Along the river, a bit of sky— ravens overhead alerting a mother bear and cubs. The clouds skim mountain peaks and treetops, trailing misty veils of rain. Fat slugs varnish the forest floor with persistent slime. Fresh, large scat: a near encounter! Fantastical mushrooms, nibbled, trampled, rotting, or in magnificent abundance . . . .—A.R.*

59

Ultimately, this remarkable rainforest and its dependent species, including the people around them, are inextricably linked like grizzly bear to salmon and forest to rain.

Coastal temperate rainforests comprise one of the most endangered forest types on Earth. Always rare, they originally covered less than 0.2 percent of the Earth's land surface. These rainforests lie at the closely linked intersections of land, estuaries, sea, and fresh water: one of the most productive living tapestries in the world. Shaped by the interplay of glacial and vibrant geological forces, the Pacific coastal rainforests of British Columbia and Alaska—with their pristine watersheds—are a non-tropical "Amazonia" that constitute more than a third of the world's remaining temperate rainforest.

In British Columbia, ancient forests cloak the slopes of the Coast Mountain Range down to the shores of the Pacific Ocean. As one of the few remaining large blocks of comparatively unmodified landscapes on Earth, the 7.4-million-hectare Great Bear encompasses the North Coast, Central Coast, and the nearby offshore archipelago of Haida Gwaii. For millennia, indigenous people have drawn physical, aesthetic, and spiritual sustenance from these rainforests and their multitude of life forms, which feature prominently in their culture and traditions.

On both the mainland and islands, the forest extends to the sea, where the indispensable wind and rain are essential for preserving the forest's makeup. Saturated marine air collides against seaside mountains, soaking the region in life-giving precipitation throughout the year. Clouds, trapped between the mountains and the sea, feed countless streams and rivers born of ancient glaciers that irrigate this primordial land. Valleys, expansive fiords, and hundreds of islands in all sizes and shapes fashion the intricate landscape. Landscape, seascape,

and weather all combine to influence the distinctive ecology of the Great Bear Rainforest.

Rivers transport sediments from glacial melt (known as "glacial flour" because of its murky appearance) which aid in the formation of wetlands and deliver nutrients to aquatic species. Downed trees embedded in streams offer hiding places and resting pools for migrating salmon in search of cool, shaded waters to spawn. Dislodged logs float downriver where they are washed ashore, anchoring the beachfront for colonizing vegetation. This exchange of nutrients and energy creates the foundation for an intricate food chain, fertile enough to provision numerous migratory and resident species.

BC's coastal temperate rainforests are characterized by some of the oldest and largest trees on Earth, the most common of which are Sitka spruce, western redcedar and western hemlock. In this lush rainforest stand 1,500-year-old cedars and 90-metre-tall spruce. It is among the world champions for carbon storage, primarily in massive tree trunks, logs on the forest floor, and thick, rich humus layers in the soil. Layers of ecosystems linked by networks of biological communities as rich and complex as any Amazonian tract—but less studied—occupy this vertical landscape.

Biologically opulent and aesthetically unique, the Great Bear Rainforest is home to thousands of species of plants, birds, and animals. Roughly 350 bird and animal species, including forty-eight species of reptiles and amphibians; twenty-five different species of trees; hundreds of species of fungi and lichens; and thousands of insects, mites, spiders, and soil organisms are found in coastal temperate rainforests.

Lichen and ferns | IVAN HUNTER

Salmon streams meander through valley bottoms, providing food for magnificent animals such as wolves, black bears, grizzlies, and the rare and mysterious spirit (Kermode) bear. Although the diversity of large mammals is generally low, some species such as grizzly bears attain exceptional densities owing to a superabundant food source—salmon—and relatively high levels of intact forest. The diverse and pristine environments of the forest are also ideal year-round habitat for many birds, including bald eagles, Queen Charlotte goshawks, and marbled murrelets.

The Great Bear Rainforest is extraordinarily rich in flora as well as fauna, including lichens, liverworts, mosses, epiphytes (canopy-dwelling plants), and soil and canopy invertebrates that live in the tallest of tree-top gardens—all species well adapted to cool and persistent moisture, complex forest canopies, and rich soils. Biological diversity of some groups in these temperate rainforests—especially invertebrates, fungi, and soil organisms—compares favourably with that of tropical rainforests. Notably, this area may support the highest fungal and lichen diversity of any forest system in the world.

The Great Bear Rainforest and Haida Gwaii provide one of the last opportunities for studying the outcome of long-term evolution on a geographic scale and for observing highly specialized and coevolved interactions that are being replaced elsewhere with invasive species or intensively managed landscapes. Because much of this area is still relatively pristine compared with other regions, it presents one of the last chances on the planet to conserve large and expansive lands in their natural state. Sadly, many of the biologically rich valley-bottom, old-growth forests have been logged or leased for logging, putting in great peril the delicate interactions of this unique biosphere.

Ultimately, this remarkable rainforest and its dependent species, including the people around them, are inextricably linked like grizzly bear to salmon and forest to rain. If we allow the remaining intact coastal temperate rainforests and the vulnerable species within them to drift toward oblivion, nature will suffer irreplaceable losses, including the rainforest giants that sprang from tiny seedlings when indigenous people and the earliest European explorers first paid homage to their splendour.

DR. PAUL C. PAQUET has served as Raincoast's senior scientist for more than twelve years. He is an adjunct professor at the Universities of Calgary, Manitoba, and New Brunswick, and a faculty associate at Guelph University. An authority on mammalian carnivores, Paul has written many scientific articles and books. He recently co-authored *The World of Wolves: New Perspectives on Ecology, Behaviour and Management* and *A New Era for Wolves and People: Wolf Recovery, Human Attitudes, and Policy.*

ANITA ROCAMORA is an internationally acclaimed ceramist and sculptor whose award-winning works are inspired by the exquisite engineering of nature. A longtime friend of Raincoast, her volunteer work on behalf of nature and wildlife takes the form of writing, illustration, sculpture, scat collection, and occasional "bon mots."

Fiordlands

DAVID McEOWN

SHERRY KIRKVOLD

Canadian artist David McEown has used the medium of watercolour for the past twenty-five years to explore and express many of the Earth's disappearing wilderness areas. His paintings—from Antarctica to the North Pole—are represented in collections worldwide.

David is a graduate of the Ontario College of Art and Design and is an elected member of the Canadian Society of Painters in Water Colour, which in 2005 awarded him the society's prestigious A.J. Casson Medal. He is a sought-after teacher and has conducted workshops and multi-media presentations for numerous art societies and museums sharing his reverence for nature and passion for the creative act of painting. When not sketching penguins down south or filming grizzly bears in Alaska, David can be found painting among the lush mosses of Pacific Spirit Park alongside his home in Vancouver, BC.

>
Great Bear Rainforest
Watercolour
61 x 92 cm

COLLIN ELDER

BEN FOX

Collin began painting two years ago, after leaving the realm of ecological conservation, which, along with a degree in wildlife biology, has focused his artwork on our deep and enigmatic connections with the natural world. His work is a transition from conservation and our relationship to the past into an expression of redesigning reality—embracing the interdependent nature of our connections with all life. Collin's paintings reflect a yearning to show how the health of our human community relies on those connections.

Hoping to evoke a vivid sense of direct experience, he paints stories of our reciprocity with the fluid and ever-changing natural landscape. These stories reveal an ancient desire to heal spiritual amnesia and reunite our mental concepts with our bodily awareness, grounding them in the living world. The paintings look through our investigations, classifications, sciences, and technologies into active, subjective participation with an integral, holistic, and mysterious ecosystem.

>
Shed Light
Oil on canvas
91 x 122 cm

MURRAY PHILLIPS

MARK HOBSON

Murray is a readily recognizable and well-known Canadian artist. Although he has been painting for over forty years, much of his life has been lived in the halls of academia. He holds graduate degrees in theology and cultural anthropology and has taught in a variety of colleges and universities for more than twenty years. His many interests include classical guitar and sailing, but an abiding love has been his yearning to paint. Murray has a strong desire to express the spiritual in his paintings. He transports his studio by canoe, sailboat, or tent trailer and spends several months each year camping in isolated areas. His paintings reflect his love for nature.

Murray is presently working on a book of his paintings advocating a renewed connection with the wilderness and its inhabitants. He also is frequently asked to speak on our relationship with both art and the wilderness.

>
The Tangled Tree
Acrylic on canvas
56 x 71 cm

We are at a critical crossroad, and our choice of path will determine the quality of existence not only for generations of humans but for flora and fauna as well. In all of my years, I have never felt more alive than standing in a wild Kynoch Inlet estuary approaching dusk. I carried the vibration of that pristine and perfect place home with me, and I feel that I have been changed on a cellular level by that experience, simply by being there. The path that sustains and supports this sacred life is the flag that I fly. My country is one where we preserve, protect, and honour the land and all that it encompasses for generations to come.

MAE MOORE

KAJ R. SVENSSON

Known mostly for her music, Mae Moore writes songs that evoke connection to place and to the personal. With two Juno nominations, two SOCAN awards, two Canadian Folk Music Award nominations, and many chart successes, Mae's career has found her songs played in major movie soundtracks, on television, and on the radio. Mae recently released *Folklore… a book of art and music*. To promote it, Mae took the train from Vancouver to Halifax and back—12,000 kilometres of Canadian inspiration.

Prior to her career as a musician, Mae studied art at Algonquin College in Ottawa and throughout the years has shown and sold her mostly expressionist Canadian landscape paintings in several BC galleries, including Red Tree Gallery on Pender Island where she lives. Her influences include other Canadian landscape artists, most notably Doris McCarthy and the Group of Seven.

> *Estuary at Kynoch Inlet*
Acrylic on canvas
91 x 91 cm

DORSET NORWICH-YOUNG

KERRI MALONE

Dorset Norwich-Young is an honours graduate of Vancouver's Emily Carr University of Art + Design. She makes her home on Pender Island where her love of nature and the outdoors has been elevated to new heights. She has signature status with the Federation of Canadian Artists and has strong ties to the Victoria and Pender Island art communities. She painted first in oils, then watercolours, and now in acrylics. Her passion for the beauty and wildness of the BC coast shows in her painting, and she presently favours large-format landscapes and seascapes as well as florals, boats, and animals.

Dorset participated in two previous very successful art-related campaigns: the Carmanah Valley and Tsitika Robson Bight. The past two summers have led her to explore BC's northern coast on what have become life-altering trips. She is strongly committed to making the Raincoast campaign as successful as her previous ones.

>
Three Sisters
Acrylic on canvas
122 x 122 cm

Since I was a child, entering the forest has filled me with wonder. In this sanctuary I become drawn close to the heart of creation and aware of how the ancient forest's timeless beauty, strength, and resilience leads me into communion with divine creative energy.

LINDA DAYAN FRIMER

MARK HOBSON

Linda is an award-winning artist, cultural facilitator, and environmental champion. Born in the gold-mining town of Wells, BC, she has created art since childhood. Absorbing the impact of stories overheard of the Second World War, she retreated to the forested world surrounding her home. The worlds of culture and nature were inseparable as she sought to protect the spirit within them. She co-authored a book, *In Honor of Our Grandmothers*, and co-founded the Gesher Holocaust project.

Working in watercolour, acrylic, and oil, her murals hang in synagogues and hospitals. Commissions and donations include Vancouver General Hospital, Children's Hospital, Canadian Cancer Foundation, and the AIDS Memorial Project. Her paintings have benefited the Western Canada Wilderness Committee, Trans Canada Trail, Canadian Red Cross, and Raincoast Conservation Foundation and have helped to raise invaluable funds. More importantly, they have an emotional impact that can create real change.

>
Tree of Life-Giving
Oil on canvas
102 x 76 cm

Cetology

The grizzled male whale
retreats from his harem
(so says Melville, I think),
or is he ousted?
Barnacles of centuries
voyage with him
solitary swimmer with wisdom in depths.
He does not reminisce,
ancient schoolmaster without disciples,
each one a silent Socrates
fixing a glaucoma'd eye on the moon.
Is this where he tells his stories
(Pacific Ocean, Hecate Strait),
spouting luminescence?
Flukes tapping, feeling the water,
sensitive fingertips of the blind,
he lusts after no one, sings
love songs for light
lyrics for deepest soundings
pastorals for tropical calms.

J. IRIBARNE

BRIAN FALCONER

Whale Soup

Top: Humpback tail | JAMEN RHODES
Centre, from left:
Humpback whale | MARK CARWARDINE
Steller sea lions | MARK CARWARDINE
Pacific white-sided dolphins | NATHAN
DE BRUYN
Below: Harbour seal | SHERRY KIRKVOLD

O n a late summer morning, *Achiever* is drifting silently—all engines and electronics off save the hydrophone, an under-water microphone. The crew scans in all directions, but the surface of the ocean yields no clue as to what is happening below. Suddenly the silence is filled by a wild sound coming from the speaker—a low howl. One of the crew whispers: "It's like a haunted freight train."

The howls grow louder and higher in pitch. Large bubbles break the surface describing a large circle about 20 to 30 metres in diameter. We unconsciously hold our breath. The sound becomes a powerful, loud wail and we, researchers and whales alike, all exhale at once as a silver cloud of herring erupts ahead of thirteen huge humpback whales lung-ing halfway out of the water with gigantic mouths wide open. Silver rivers flow out as their mighty jaws close on a breakfast of fat Pacific herring. Our spontaneous shouts dissipate out over the water while the whales rest at the surface. They arch their backs high, throw their powerful seven-tonne tails into the air, and disappear into the depths, leaving behind thirteen polished footprints and silence.

It is a magnificent ritual performed year in and year out by the same whales, a club if you like—one of only two known in Canada—

Aboard Raincoast's research vessel, Achiever, *a team of scientists and observers worked, ate, and slept on rotations for one to two months at a time. They recorded observations of marine mammals in the waters between Dixon Entrance and Vancouver Island. Tracklines were set across Hecate and Queen Charlotte Straits and into inlets along the Central and North Coasts. In total, Raincoast traversed more than 14,000 kilometres at sea and recorded more than 2,300 sightings of marine mammals.*

whose members we recognize from unique markings on their tails. Swimming each year from their Hawaiian or Mexican breeding and calving grounds, they gather at the same sites to feed cooperatively on huge shoals of herring. Over and over the pattern is repeated—surfacing in unison—every few minutes and every few hundred metres.

Reluctantly, we head out into Hecate Strait in pursuit of our real goal, to photo-identify fin whales, but first we are sidetracked by two large groups of the salmon-eating resident killer whales (orcas) slipping by almost unnoticed. These waters have been considered for critical habitat designation under SARA (Species at Risk Act) for both northern resident killer whales and humpback whales.

Fin whales are the second largest whale in the world, only slightly smaller than a blue whale. Like humpback whales, they and most other species were mercilessly hunted until the 1960s, nearly to extinction. The humpback whale is a rare conservation success story. Populations have recovered significantly, a testament to what human restraint can achieve. Fin whales appear to be making a slow recovery, and they concentrate in this area at this time of the year. We want to learn more about their numbers and feeding habits.

On this rare calm day in Hecate Strait, there are sporadic reports from the platform: two harbour seals, five Dall's porpoises, a few distant humpbacks, and a constant array of seabirds. Then an exuberant shout:

"Orcas!" We are thrilled that they are a large group of rarely seen offshore killer whales. Methodically, we photo-identify each individual, adding to a database of information from these unusual encounters. Besides an apparent preference for sharks, little is known of their diet.

On our way to more sheltered waters, we swing by a small group of islands and confirm a report of a raft of sixty or more sea otters in a kelp-strewn bay. Reintroduced after being hunted out completely from this coast, their population is also recovering. This is the most northerly sighting to date on the BC coast.

Re-entering the sound, we head for "the racetrack," a place where for the last five days we have encountered fin whales feeding. The late afternoon sun highlights a huge column of mist. From the platform: "Blow, dead ahead, 2,000 metres. Fin whale." Snubbing the dozen or so humpbacks feeding in the area, we spend the next four hours identifying six fin whales.

Later at anchor, we go over the last two days. Yesterday, there were:

- an estimated 300 Pacific white-sided dolphins;
- a group of nine transient (Bigg's) killer whales, launching into the air in pursuit of mammalian prey;
- an islet covered with about 160 Steller (Northern) sea lions;
- ten Dall's porpoises racing like green flares in the bioluminescence as we steamed to our anchorage.

Killer whale | IAN JANSMA

As we chat, I remark that what we have seen in two days represents more marine mammals than most people see in a lifetime. Elephant seals, minke whales, harbour porpoises, and occasionally other species are also known to this area.

The mood becomes somber as conversation turns to oil tankers. Our study area is right in the middle of the proposed tanker route from a terminal proposed for Kitimat. If approved, a year-round procession of monolithic tankers loaded with toxic bitumen and other chemicals would run right through these rich waters.

The discussion turns to impacts. The path of the bubble-net-feeding humpbacks was a series of dots a few hundred metres apart—back and forth across the traffic lanes. "The racetrack" is located right on the "white line" of the proposed tanker route and stretches from shore to shore across the narrow channel.

We talk of noise from the 8-metre propellers and huge engines and of the disruption of communication and feeding. We have recently learned that humpback whales sing in this area. In one of the great mysteries of nature, all whales in an area learn the same song each year, which is different from the previous year. One thought is that they compose their new song in these quiet waters.

But the main topic is the unspeakable tragic consequences of an oil spill from a tanker accident.

We retreat into silence, too troubled by the conversation to speak anymore. As I sip my Scotch, one of the research crew adds quietly: "It's whale soup out there." We all understand that every marine mammal we have seen over the last days would be reached by a spill within a matter of hours—an unimaginable toll.

BRIAN FALCONER has headed Raincoast's Marine Operations Program for more than a decade, overseeing the operation of *Achiever*, the organization's research vessel. A pioneer in boat-based ecotourism, Brian has a long history of captaining vessels on the BC and Alaska coasts. He restored the schooner *Maple Leaf*, originally built in 1904. As Raincoast's guide outfitter coordinator, Brian lead the foundation's recent acquisition of a commercial hunting tenure which encompasses the heart of spirit bear territory.

HUMPBACK TAIL

KEVIN JOHNSON

KAJ R. SVENSSON

Born in London, Ontario, Kevin is a self-taught pencil artist who now resides on Quadra Island, located off the northeast coast of Vancouver Island. He retired from a career in the Canadian Forces that took him to every corner of the world, but it is here on the West Coast of Canada that Kevin finds the inspiration for his works of art. He strives to create photo-realistic detail in his pieces by relying on texture and tonal values of the subjects. Kevin, an avid photographer and kayaker, hopes to convey his deep appreciation for the beauty of the natural world around him through his art.

>
For Generations
to Come—Sea Otters
Pencil on illustration
board
23 x 34 cm

Txeemsim's Trickery, acrylic painting on birch. Txeemsim, the raven, is a trickster. He has a sun in his mouth indicating he is stealing the sun for the world. Enbridge is also a trickster. They are spending millions in advertising to "trick" us into believing they have the "light" and that this "light" is prosperity. Enbridge is a schemer, very much like Txeemsim was in his heyday. Indigenous nations worldwide know in their hearts that if they harm their environment, they harm themselves. There is no trickery in that.

TODD STEPHENS

VIVIAN STEPHENS

Todd Stephens was born in Gitlaxdax (Terrace, BC) in 1988 to the House of Gitlaxaylibit of Sim'oogit Siispaguut and Sim'oogit Ni'isyuus of the Killerwhale Tribe, from the old village of Git'iks. His Nisga'a name is Hlgu Śk'an Milksim Ts'im Aks, given to him at the age of eight by his maternal great-grandmother. His interest in Nisga'a art began at age fourteen, while watching his uncle Albert Stephens transfer a design to watercolour paper to be ready for painting. From that time he has continued to draw the ideas that flow to him.

Todd graduated from the Freda Diesing School of Northwest Coast Art's Fine Arts Diploma program in 2009. He won the YVR Art Foundation Scholarship Award in 2008 and 2010. This award enabled him to showcase a hummingbird headdress ('09–'10) and a salmon drum with a carved salmon drumstick ('11–'12).

>
Unheard Voices
Acrylic on canvas
Diptych
41 x 60 cm

ALAN WYLIE

MARK HOBSON

Born in Glasgow, Scotland, in 1938, Alan graduated from Glasgow School of Art in 1960 with a degree in mural design and mosaics. He immigrated to Nova Scotia in 1967 and became a full-time artist, teacher, and art gallery owner. In 1974 he moved to British Columbia and now lives in Fort Langley with his artist wife, Janice Robertson.

Alan has had seventy-four solo shows. He is a senior signature member of the Northwest Watercolor Society; the California Watercolor Association; the Louisiana Watercolor Society; the Canadian Society of Painters in Water Colour; and the Federation of Canadian Artists, receiving their Lifetime Achievement Award in 2007. He is also a dolphin fellow of the American Watercolor Society (the first Canadian to achieve this distinction). He served as juror for the 139th *Annual International Exhibition* of the American Watercolor Society in New York, and was made an honourary member of the Jiangsu Watercolour Research Institute, Nanjing, China.

>
Sea Lion Drive By
Oil on canvas
51 x 122 cm

To touch the realm of the supernatural, where travel in water is as in air, one must first achieve pureness of body and mind through fasting, drinking salt water, and bathing in the sea. The most powerful underwater Supernatural Being, a being with both human spirit and form, wears the cloak of Killer Whale—SGaan. This lone matriarch's dorsal fin breaks the barrier between two worlds.

Our challenge is to protect the magic of Myth Time by treading lightly on the natural world, the plane that connects us to the spirit of our ancestors—to maintain balance on the edge of the earth.

APRIL WHITE

JACK LITRELL

"From inspiration through conception of my art…it's as if I am experiencing innate memories that connect me deeply to my cultural past. It's as if my brain is doing the seeing, not my eyes. The feeling of this cerebral vision is supernatural…magical."

April White received her BSc from UBC and worked as a field geologist, rendering the natural world into maps and honing her inherent artistic inclination. Formally named SGaana Jaad (Killerwhale Woman) in potlatch, she is a descendant of the renowned Haida Stastas Eagle Chief and artist Charles Edenshaw and weaver Isabella Edenshaw, and a member of the Yahgu'jaanaas Raven Clan. Born on Haida Gwaii, April honours her heritage as she interprets the natural and mythological world. Self-taught, she creates art conscious of the knife-edge balance of life—with her ancestors, she believes you must watch every step or fall off the edge of the Earth.

>
Realm of the Supernatural
Watercolour and acrylic
58 x 76 cm

My otter bowl was inspired when I spent a whole day watching an otter play and dive. Often he would come within a few feet of me…his big eyes looking right at me, dancing his dance for me. I thought about how simple his life was compared to ours; he only needed what was around him. I think he was trying to tell me that it was up to me, to us humans, to protect his home…our home. Carving him was a way of passing on his message.

CAROL YOUNG BAGSHAW

Carol is a descendent of the Eagles of Haida Gwaii, and her clan is the Tsiij git'anee.

In 2009 she attended the Freda Diesing School of Northwest Coast Art under the direction of world-renowned carvers Ken McNeil, Stan Bevan, and Dempsey Bob. She is forever grateful to her instructors and peers for sharing their knowledge and passion for the art.

For thousands of years the land, ocean, and sky have provided for us, and now it is time for the people to give back, be grateful, and protect these gifts we have been given. Carol's role as a Haida woman and artist is to do just that. Carving alder and cedar, she carves the eagles, whales, ravens, salmon, otters, frogs, bears, etc., that are part of her; they are her family. We are all connected, and we all need each other to survive on this beautiful Earth.

>
Otter Bowl
Red alder
14 x 39 x 15 cm

KINDRIE GROVE

Kindrie Grove is a Penticton artist, art educator, and author. Her often large-scale paintings and bronze sculptures express her reverence and love for animals, both wild and domestic. Formal training at the Alberta College of Art + Design has led to her successful career as a professional artist. Kindrie's studio is a gallery where her work can be viewed and is also a classroom where she teaches a variety of workshops and courses. Her work is currently featured in galleries across Canada and in numerous international private and corporate collections, including the Toronto Congress Centre's "Kindrie Grove Wing." She lives with her husband, Michael, and young son, Kellen, in the wild hills of the Okanagan Valley, British Columbia.

>
Free Floating
Oil on canvas
61 x 122 cm

Tide Lines

There is a place on shore where a line becomes a
question, a mirror for the sky. The tide walk—a
place for ghosts, lost in spray, steps measured by
slick shells and the flitting shapes of shorebirds.

    one feather
    carried through the haze
    a gull's cry

Pinned between the forest's edge and the crashing
surf. A middle-land of drying froth—parallel,
liminal, smooth as feathers from a raven's wing.
A highway for us to walk, tired and without
footsteps, the thinning edge of the world.

PATRICK M. PILARSKI

CAROLINE FOX

Flocking to the Coast

F ramed by the ancient rainforests of Haida Gwaii and the Great Bear, the productive waters of the British Columbia coast support multitudes of marine birds—the stunningly diverse and conspicuous creatures of marine ecosystems. In waters that one day lie still as a lake and the next tower with tumbling waves looming more than 10 metres high, millions of marine birds live out their lives. Predators and scavengers of the ocean's surface, deep-sea divers, and roamers of this ragged coastline, they are a wild and opportunistic lot. Perhaps the most famous are albatrosses and puffins, but marine birds are a colourful and incredibly rich assemblage of species. Commonly grouped as seabirds, marine waterfowl, marine raptors, and shorebirds, more than 150 species are supported by the British Columbian coast. Tens of millions of these birds pulse through its coastal waters each year, with a smaller portion residing year round.

In the offshore waters—once believed to be the realm of sea monsters and other mythical beings—it is the pelagic seabirds that rule. At this very moment, giant albatrosses glide over the ocean's surface, just a few nautical miles off the British Columbia coast. Their internal odometers, some logging more than a million miles, measure a life spent almost entirely out on the ocean, among giant rollers and sea

91

Top: Northern fulmar | MIKE YIP
Centre, left to right: Glaucous-winged gulls | GUILLAUME MAZILLE
Greater yellowlegs | MARIE O'SHAUGHNESSY
Below: Tufted puffin | MIKE YIP

The list of human impacts on marine birds is a lengthy one and includes introduced predators on colonies, conflict and competition with fisheries, climate change, over-harvesting, habitat destruction, and more. Marine birds are also incredibly susceptible to oil and are often the most prominent and abundant victims of oil spills; it just takes one drop to kill a bird.

foam. Three species of albatross—with wingspans that stretch more than 2 metres—visit this coast. They mix with massive flocks of sooty shearwaters, the lean greyhounds of the sea that arrive following a giant, migratory sweep of the Pacific Ocean from breeding grounds in the Southern Hemisphere. Northern fulmars, in mottled shades of ashy grey to brilliant white, visit the coast in large numbers following their breeding period in the North; they too join with the shearwaters and albatrosses offshore.

Many marine birds visit BC's coast, never once alighting on land, but for others it is a breeding destination. On a shore strewn with thousands of islands and a jagged coastline, millions of birds breed here each year. In spring and early summer, seabirds—including tufted puffins, common murres, Cassin's and rhinoceros auklets—can be found breeding in more than five hundred colonies along the coast. Some prefer tightly packed, guano-encrusted islands that at a distance appear to loom like icebergs out of the sea, while others take a more stealthy approach and breed in the lush grasses or among the roots of stunted spruce trees on scattered, windswept islands. Triangle Island, located just off the northern tip of Vancouver Island, is the largest colony in Canada's Pacific Coast waters and currently hosts more than two million breeding seabirds.

Some fledgling marine birds, like common murres, make a single, spirally leap off sheer precipices into rough waters before beginning a life spent at sea. Ancient murrelets do something else entirely. Known by some as "the running of the murrelets," tens of thousands of downy ancient murrelet chicks follow nocturnal, tumbling paths off the forested islands of Haida Gwaii to the dark ocean where they reunite with their singing parents, swim rapidly offshore, and then spend several months flightless and vulnerable at sea. Others, including fuzzy, wobbly-legged black oystercatcher chicks, make a more gradual transition to a marine life.

In contrast to the millions of seabirds that breed in British Columbia, comparatively few marine waterfowl (geese and ducks) or shorebirds breed along this coast, with many preferring areas to the north, such as the Arctic, as well as the continent's interior. Still, that pattern does not detract from the tremendous importance of the coast and its resources to marine waterfowl and shorebirds. For example, each year, large aggregations of these birds gather at Pacific herring spawn events. Black brant, surf and white-winged scoters refuel on energy-dense herring eggs, while overhead, lines of geese and ducks streak north after overwintering in more sheltered waters to the south, including the Salish Sea. The majority of the world's population of western sandpipers migrates along the coast, to and from breeding grounds in the North. Hundreds of thousands of these sandpipers—British Columbia's most abundant shorebird—can be found at stop-over sites, where the tiny, rapidly moving sandpipers run over the flats in great synchronized movements and lick up vast quantities of intertidal biofilm.

It seemed strange the first time I saw it, but after several encounters, the sight of gleaming white, Arctic-breeding snow geese flying

Black-footed albatross | MIKE YIP

dozens of miles offshore against a marine backdrop filled with waves and Hawaiian-breeding black-footed albatrosses made it clear that this coast supports a diversity of marine birds in all manner of ways. As a coastal refueling station and place to overwinter, breed, forage, raise young, molt feathers, and simply wander, the BC coast supports all critical phases in the life of a marine bird. The trouble is, these life phases all ultimately rely upon healthy, functioning ecosystems.

Despite their multitudes, their diversity and the seeming robustness of their lives, many marine birds are of urgent conservation concern—especially the seabirds. After ten months spent surveying marine birds at sea, Raincoast counted nearly 100,000 individuals belonging to seventy species. Nearly 10 percent were already considered to be at risk of extinction, while more species continue to join the ranks of those warranting an assessment. The list of human impacts on marine birds is a lengthy one and includes introduced predators on colonies, conflict and competition with fisheries, climate change, over-harvesting, habitat destruction, and more. Marine birds are also incredibly susceptible to oil and are often the most prominent and abundant victims of oil spills; it just takes one drop to kill a bird.

With rampant modification and degradation of coastal zones around the world, the British Columbian coast remains an important and productive refuge for a unique assemblage of marine birds. Keeping this part of the coast oil free represents a significant step towards protecting marine birds now and for the future.

CAROLINE FOX is a biologist with Raincoast Conservation Foundation and is currently completing her PhD in biology at the University of Victoria. Caroline's research revolves around coastal ecology and conservation and includes studies of birds, bears, kelp forests, and forage fishes. Marine birds, the spectacular members of marine ecosystems, are a longtime interest.

93

MARK HOBSON

MURRAY PHILLIPS

Mark Hobson lives in Tofino, BC, where he has painted professionally for over twenty-five years. Mark is best known for his passionate portrayals of the remote Pacific Coast. Whether it be pounding surf, misty coves, rainforests, or the underwater realm, the careful use of light is always present, enhancing subtle drama in his work. Trained as a biologist, he taught high school science before devoting his time to painting in watercolours, oils, and acrylics. Mark's work has won awards in the USA, Canada, and Europe.

A strong advocate for preserving the wilderness he loves to paint, Mark has devoted countless hours and works to environmental campaigns. After he brought artists to Carmanah Valley on Vancouver Island in 1989, a new provincial park was established. It is his vision and organizational skills that have brought this group of artists together to challenge the threat of oil tankers on the northern BC coast.

>
Pelagic Cormorants:
Diving for Gobies
Acrylic on canvas
91 x 36 cm

Marbled Murrelet in laboured Lift-off

W. ALLAN HANCOCK

KAJ R. SVENSSON

W. Allan Hancock's fascination with the natural world began in his childhood and has found expression in his artwork ever since. While the subject of Allan's art continues to be the beauty of the natural world, many of his paintings offer a reminder of the impact we have on it.

Allan's art career began in 1989 when he started to work as a wildlife artist for a greeting card company. Drawn to its natural beauty and abundant wildlife, Allan moved to Vancouver Island in 1995 to pursue a self-employed art career. Since then Allan's artwork has been selected for numerous fundraising projects for wildlife and habitat conservation purposes. His work has appeared twice on the Canadian Wildlife Habitat Conservation Stamp, and two books exclusively feature Allan's paintings. Allan hopes his work inspires each viewer to take a closer look at the natural world and to treasure all that it offers.

>
Swell for Now—
Tufted Puffin
Acrylic on board
61 x 76 cm

JANICE ROBERTSON

MARK HOBSON

Janice Robertson launched her career as a professional artist in 1989. She has received many awards over the years and is currently represented by five commercial galleries. Janice is a signature member of the Federation of Canadian Artists, Landscape Artists International, and the Northwest Watercolor Society. She served as president of the Federation of Canadian Artists from 1999 to 2001 and is listed in *Who's Who in Canada*. Janice's paintings are in collections throughout the world, and she is a popular and well-respected workshop instructor now living in the historic village of Fort Langley, BC, with her artist husband, Alan Wylie.

"I love to paint light and the beauty of simple things. After over twenty-five years of painting, I am still learning and discovering new ways of expression. It is a privilege to be able to make a living at something that I find so joyful. I am very grateful."

>
Fly By
Acrylic on canvas
76 x 102 cm

CARL CHAPLIN

JONATHAN DY

Carl Chaplin has been painting wildlife for the last sixty years. Although his training was in science, he pursued his love of art. In 1970 he moved to BC to be closer to the wilderness and further from civilization. Over the years Carl's images have been donated to many worthwhile causes and millions of reproductions have been distributed worldwide.

Although his technique is modern, he is a super-traditionalist using the ancient principles of the Golden Ratio (Phi). He developed a unique method within Phi called "Reiteration." Rather than a sketch, a very small painting is created. That first iteration is enlarged and completely repainted, adding more detail. The process is repeated and results in a series of paintings. His most recent development has been to paint in stereoscopic 3D. Having toured around the world many years ago, Carl is now a non-flying, non-driving, stay-at-home-and-paint-all-day kind of guy.

>
Manifest Destiny
Acrylic on canvas
91 x 122 cm

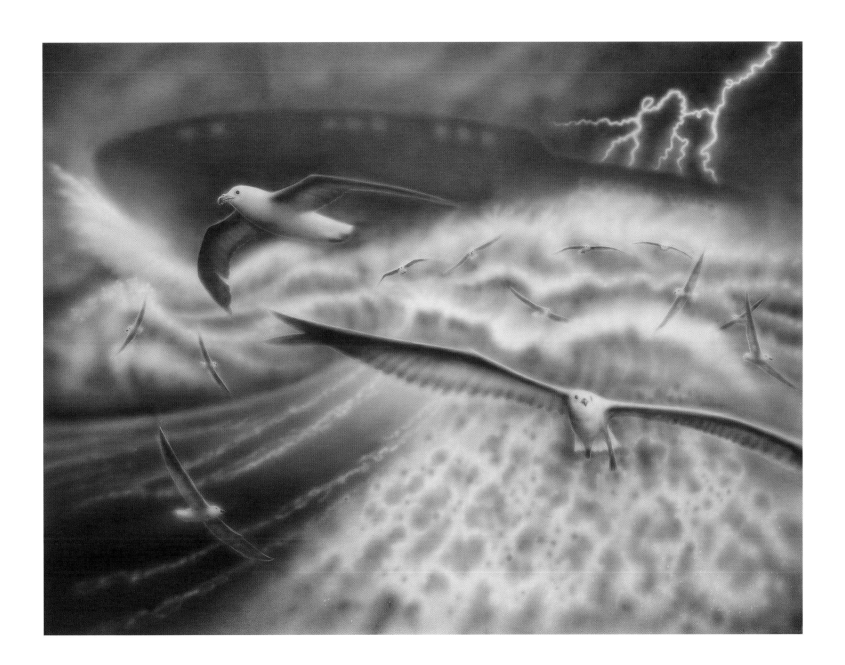

BRENT COOKE

KAJ R. SVENSSON

Born in 1947 in Vancouver, BC, Brent discovered a love of carving at a young age, starting with wood relief, figures, stone carvings, and fine-detail decoys. In recent years he has also entered the bronze-casting field. The bronze works Brent produces are cast at Valley Bronze of Oregon, a foundry of fine repute that delivers consistently high calibre art of all sizes.

Brent's work focuses on birds and sea creatures for the most part, with birds of prey being his favourite subjects. His pieces feature very fine detailing, and most represent a chase, the outcome of which is left to the viewer's imagination. His use of negative space and ability to capture the essence of movement and interaction of his subjects has been widely complimented by art lovers at galleries and shows. Brent's studio (CastArt Studio) is located in Victoria, BC.

>
Touchdown
Bufflehead duck
Bronze, black
granite base
40 x 56 x 28 cm

Eight Storeys High 250 Metres Down

Millions of years ago Earth was Ocean
and two *über*continents, shelved
by a single silica sponge reef stretching hemispheres,
the only glass in existence
giving birth to a planet's future.

Glass reefs: extinct for 40 million years…
Merely a scientist, I glance again at a photograph
deep down in the Danube Valley—a monastery, dwarfed
by high cliffs where pale fossilized reefs
                    hang
                            in the sky.

In Spain, there is a castle built upon glass.
What was once alive under the sea now stares blankly
through air. Shrubbery frames what used to hide fishes,
their beautiful colours, their elegant fins.

At last a day dawns
when living glass reefs 9,000 years old
are found eight storeys tall
off Canada's west coast. I squeeze into a submarine
built for two, shrugging off my claustrophobia
plunge into Hecate Strait
press my forehead against the window.
250 metres down, I meet my dinosaurs face to face,
alive.

                            CHRISTINE LOWTHER

CAROLINE FOX

What Lies Below

Top: Sea pen | DANE STABEL

Centre, left to right:

Smooth velvet snail | TOM REIMCHEN

Kelp forest | COLIN BATES

Wolf eel | DANE STABEL

Below: White-lined dirona | TOM REIMCHEN

Far from the monotonous blue of modern nautical charts, the ocean and the corrugated coastlines it forms with the lands of the Great Bear Rainforest and Haida Gwaii are incredibly diverse. Visible from space, the surface of the ocean streaks and swirls in gradients of temperature and chlorophyll, a fundamental photosynthetic pigment and a common proxy for biological productivity. Cut through by the fins of sharks and killer whales, coloured by phytoplankton, and mixed by winds, the ocean's varied surface merely hints at the complicated, fragile, and unique life that lies under the sea. Beneath the waves are vibrant ecological communities, including fine-silt estuaries; surf-pounded rocky intertidal zones; sea vents; and deep, dark, mud-filled gullies lying just off the continental shelf break. Inhabiting these communities are extraordinary marine organisms, some of which are found nowhere else in the world.

Part of what drives the rich and unique diversity of life on this coast is its tremendous spatial variability. As the crow flies, the British Columbia coast measures less than 1,000 kilometres, but in actual length it stretches nearly 30,000 kilometres. Carved out by glaciers that retreated some ten thousand years ago, this coast is as jagged as

105

Another driver of life on this coast is the tide. Climbing up and down the intertidal twice a day, the tidal movements of the ocean create a unique zone where species thrive in an environment of extremes: pounded by surf one moment and bathed by freshwater rain the next; baked in the hot sun and later cooled as the tide rises over them.

they come, providing a rich mosaic of habitat types across the coastal seascape.

Spatial variability is just one driver of the diversity of coastal life. Just as terrestrial ecosystems shift with the seasons—deciduous trees drop their leaves in fall and bears hibernate for the winter—seasonal changes in light and temperature also affect the variability and diversity of life on this coast. Currents are another major force driving coastal marine ecosystems. The North Pacific Current runs eastward across the Pacific Ocean, now bringing debris from the 2011 Japanese tsunami along with it, and splits along the British Columbia coast. Butting up against the continental shelf, this current forces cool, nutrient-rich water to the surface. This upwelling current is one of the main reasons why BC's coastal waters are so productive and filled with a diversity of life that includes whales, seabirds, fishes, and kelp forests.

From these clear, cold, and nutrient-rich waters, spring breaks out on the coast with the first phytoplankton bloom. In the upper layers of the coastal ocean and way out past the shelf break, tiny drifting photosynthetic organisms soak up sunlight and carbon dioxide to produce oxygen and complex carbon molecules—the building blocks of life. Rapidly multiplying, miniscule diatoms and dinoflagellates turn the surface waters a rusty, murky hue. In some years, calcium-plated coccolithophores dominate the phytoplankton community and turn the ocean's surface milky white, often over such large areas that their blooms can be monitored by orbiting satellites. Zooplankton, which includes copepods and larval fishes, increase in abundance as they graze on phytoplankton; in turn, krill and fishes prey upon zooplankton. The species we typically identify with marine ecosystems—including killer whales, salmon, tuna, and tufted puffins—are positioned as higher-level predators, fueled by a complex, fragile, and highly dynamic food web.

Not all photosynthetic life forming the base of the food chain on this coast is phytoplankton. In the nearshore, kelp forests fringe a substantial proportion of the British Columbian coastline and are one of the most productive and diverse ecosystems on the planet. Nursery grounds to juvenile salmon, herring, and rockfish; fuel for a large proportion of the nearshore food web; and exporters of huge tangled rafts of kelp to the offshore, kelp forests provide a suite of services to the surrounding environment. Further up the inlets, in sheltered bays and estuaries, spears of eelgrass bend in the current and juvenile fishes dart back and forth, moving from cover to feed. Similar to kelp forests, eelgrass meadows are highly productive and species rich, providing important habitat, resources, and nursery grounds for many species, including Dungeness crabs and salmon.

Another driver of life on this coast is the tide. Climbing up and down the intertidal twice a day, the tidal movements of the ocean create a unique zone where species thrive in an environment of extremes: pounded by surf one moment and bathed by freshwater rain the next; baked in the hot sun and later cooled as the tide rises over them. Ranging from the wave-pounded rocky outershore—where predatory sea stars pry open giant mussels and where nudibranchs

Red Irish lord | TOM REIMCHEN

(sea slugs) graze on multi-hued sponges—to sandy beaches inhabited by razor clams, purple shore crabs, and worms, the intertidal zone encompasses a vast swath of habitat types and a diversity of creatures that are adapted, quite literally, to life on the edge. The coastal saying "When the tide goes out, the table is set" speaks to the importance of the intertidal as a food resource for people but also for a number of wildlife species.

The intertidal zone, eelgrass meadows, and kelp forests of the nearshore are inundated with light, but much of the coastal ocean consists of deep water and darkness, where sunlight never reaches. Following the glacial-tilled trenches of the inlets westward, out over the continental shelf, the seafloor drops away. Annelids churn the mud like earthworms of the sea; rockfish and halibut roam over the ocean's bottom; and copious amounts of plankton, fecal matter, and other detritus drift down from the light-filled surface waters as marine snow. In the depths of Hecate Strait and Queen Charlotte Sound, pale glass sponge reefs form vital habitat for a diversity of species, including endangered rockfish. Only discovered in the 1980s, the glass sponge reefs lying off the BC coast are ancient, having grown there for at least nine thousand years. Reaching more than 15 metres high and extending several hundred square kilometers over the seafloor, BC's glass sponge reefs are one of the great wonders of Canada's coastal oceans and rank among the largest biological structures on the planet.

Above the ghostly glass sponge reefs, the ocean's layers support a unique and ever-changing richness of marine life. Sharks twist in the deep waters; Pacific herring spawn on the kelps in the nearshore; and—in what cannot become reality—an Asia-bound supertanker laden with crude oil crosses the path of hunting killer whales.

Visions of the future offer two plain possibilities. The first is an oil-free coast that stands forever as one of the last great refuges for wild species and ecosystems both above and below the water's surface. In the second—a nightmarish scenario—the coast lies at risk to the ultimate environmental degradations: chronic and catastrophic oil spills.

If supertankers ply these waters, life in coastal marine ecosystems—which encompasses everything from kelps, abalones, and zooplankton to salmon, killer whales, and eulachons—would face an uncertain future with the ever-present possibility of tragic and permanent consequences.

CAROLINE FOX is a biologist with Raincoast Conservation Foundation and is currently completing her PhD in biology at the University of Victoria. Caroline's research revolves around coastal ecology and conservation and includes studies of birds, bears, kelp forests, and forage fishes. Marine birds, the spectacular members of marine ecosystems, are a longtime interest.

After the terrorist attack on the World Trade Centre in the United States, there was a belief that retaliation with violence and military force would create symmetry. Our challenge is to find new solutions for old patterns and creative ways to resolve issues that are generational, such as terrorism. Retaliation only breeds more revenge.

Sea Monster was a mythological being that floated half in the water and half in the air. In the old days, when people used canoes as a means of transportation, one of their greatest fears was to run into Sea Monster. They would travel for miles around to avoid running into t'samuus because the Sea Monster had the power to capsize canoes. Because their fear was really of the unknown, Sea Monster was a symbol of terror. Today a new terror comes from the threat posed by oil supertankers on our coast. We still fear the unknown; we still fear the Sea Monster.

ROBERT DAVIDSON

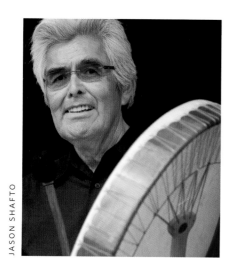

JASON SHAFTO

Robert Davidson is one of Canada's most respected and important contemporary artists. Of Haida descent, he is a master carver of totem poles and masks and also works as a printmaker, painter, and jeweller. A leading figure in the renaissance of Haida art and culture, he is renowned as an impeccable craftsman whose creative and personal interpretation of traditional Haida form is unparalleled.

Davidson's internationally acclaimed body of work is found in private and public collections including the National Gallery of Canada, the Vancouver Art Gallery, the Canadian Museum of Civilization, and the Southwest Museum in California. He holds honourary degrees from the University of Victoria, Simon Fraser University, Emily Carr Institute of Art + Design, and the Southern Methodist University in Texas. He received both the National Aboriginal Achievement Award and Order of British Columbia in 1995, and in 1996 was awarded the prestigious Order of Canada.

>
Looking at Asymmetry
Serigraph print
102 x 36 cm

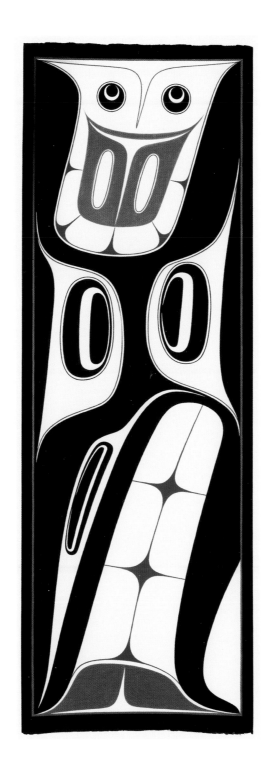

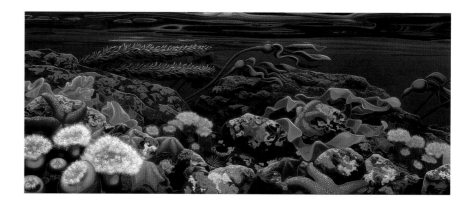

CHILI THOM

BEN FOX

Born and raised in British Columbia, Chili has enjoyed an interesting and inspired life of hiking, climbing, and exploring the vast and beautiful wilderness of the Pacific Northwest. For the past sixteen years he's been based out of Whistler and the Sea-to-Sky corridor, providing him with easy access to the outdoors and an international client base.

The amazing natural spaces and landscapes of BC inspire much of Chili's artwork. He has explored the province extensively as a professional wilderness and sea kayak guide and also as a television host. He initially began painting with acrylics in 1998 on a self-taught journey and has worked for years to develop his colours and lines into a bold and unique style that recently won him Best in Show at the 2012 Federation of Canadian Artists *Landscapes* exhibit. When not in front of the canvas, Chili expresses his creativity as a DJ or filmmaker.

>
What Lies Beneath
Acrylic on canvas
86 x 102 cm

Copper Rockfish

GAYE ADAMS

MARK HOBSON

During the three decades that have spanned Gaye's career in art, her focus has been painting what delights her most: the effects of atmosphere and light. Gaye's paintings are representational but generally rendered in a loose fashion, as understatement best suits her personality and process. It brings her great pleasure to take advantage of opportunities to travel and paint on location as frequently as her schedule allows.

Currently Gaye is working in both oil paints and in soft pastels, enjoying these mediums for their malleable and direct nature. She shows and sells her work nationally and internationally, and she also teaches both at home and abroad. In addition to being a member of the Oil Painters of America, Gaye holds senior signature status with the Federation of Canadian Artists and the Pastel Artists of Canada. She works out of her home studio in Blind Bay, BC.

>
Rockfish Garden
Oil on linen
102 x 102 cm

DIANNE BERSEA

SHERRY KIRKVOLD

Dianne's creativity began in the wild places of Canada's westernmost province. With one youthful year at Pachena Point Light Station and initially home-schooled on an emergency air base in the open grassland of the Fraser Plateau, Dianne has embraced the British Columbia wild in all its manifestations. "I've always appreciated having a close, intimate relationship with my physical and emotional landscape—living, breathing my inspiration. In the process I become part of the landscape, a silent witness to its mood and beauty."

An elected member of Canadian Society of Painters in Water Colour and signature member of Federation of Canadian Artists, Dianne's background in graphic design, fine art, natural history illustration, and exhibit design brings a wide range of knowledge and experience to her work. Emphasis on process and immediacy, strong colours, and stylized imagery are striking characteristics. Dianne lives and works on Cortes Island in the northern Gulf Islands.

>
Underwater Adagio
Watercolour
50 x 69 cm

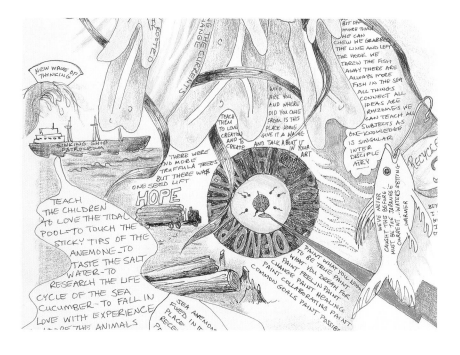

SHEILA KARROW

BEN FOX

Award-winning artist and teacher Sheila Karrow lives with her two chil-dren on Haida Gwaii in British Columbia. After completing a degree in fine art and education, Sheila spent several years teaching high school visual art and English. After ten years of full-time art making, Sheila earned a masters degree in art education and is currently teaching in the school district where she continues to share her passion for imaginative learn-ing with young children and adults.

Sheila's paintings communicate both a literal and metaphorical under-standing of the natural world. She strives for an intimate connection with the subject yet also reveals the unknowable reality of such a form. Her carefully rendered images in acrylic and watercolour reveal the intensity and interconnectedness of life.

>
A Fragile Place of Wonder
Watercolour
46 x 74 cm

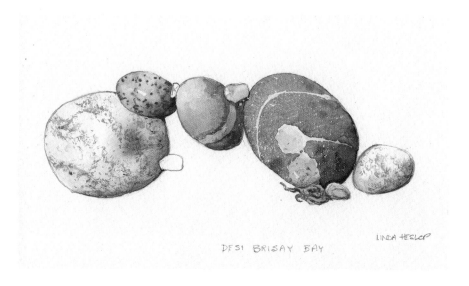

DESI BRISAY BAY   LINDA HESLOP

LINDA HESLOP

BEN FOX

Linda Heslop began drawing at a very early age, tutored by her father who was an artist and architect. Her realistic style led to work in illustration, logos, magazine covers, feature articles, and several books at an international level. This included her own book, *The Art of Caving*, an overlook of her two decades of caving. She became recognized as the most published caver artist worldwide in the 1990s and was the second recipient of the National Speleological Society's Arts and Letters Award. Linda has been a Victoria, British Columbia, resident since 1957. Now represented by Canadian Art Connections, she has turned her full attention to fine art following her love of West Coast images.

>
*Constellation
Conservations*
Watercolour
55 x 73 cm

LINDA HESLOP

Tidal Pull

I always know when you are returning

because I start dreaming

of the estuary… at work, in

long meetings all the chairs dissolve

into muck-stuck logs, slick

shadows, raw reek of lost bodies caught

on high ground, lying twisted

in creamy shells, smelling of life

and death at the same time, soft tideline tonguing

moist membranes, stroking silken

beds of kelp…helpless

against undulating fluids, salty, oozing,

penetrating every

pore, encrusting tufty mounds

of glasswort…and the whispers, oh

the never-ending whispers of

papery grasses, faster, rattling, shattering, scream

of gull overhead, spent shotgun

cartridges sinking

in brine…

time stands still, lies

flat, splayed,

dampness dangling like corpse

legs, slime mats glisten in

dimming light, blueblack water shape-

shifts, trades places with

raven's back, intergrades openly…endlessly…blameless

KIM GOLDBERG

PAUL PAQUET
ANITA ROCAMORA

A Bountiful Mixing of Oceanic and Fresh Water

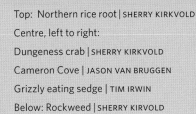

Top: Northern rice root | SHERRY KIRKVOLD
Centre, left to right:
Dungeness crab | SHERRY KIRKVOLD
Cameron Cove | JASON VAN BRUGGEN
Grizzly eating sedge | TIM IRWIN
Below: Rockweed | SHERRY KIRVOLD

B ritish Columbia's Pacific Coast is a complicated archipelago, where land and sea play hide-and-seek along the shoreline's byzantine contours. For most of the coastline, dynamic tides and immutable topography strictly define the boundaries of the aquatic environment. Diverse animals and organisms flourish, having coevolved to negotiate their survival in this remarkably complex natural community. A species' particular ecological niche has as much to do with terrain and turbulence as with sunlight, currents, and temperature.

Nowhere is this more evident than in the river mouths, bays, and inlets that comprise the coast's biologically fertile estuaries: the renowned nurseries of countless terrestrial and marine species. Unlike much of the surrounding coastline, estuaries are continually malleable owing to their sedimentary composition. Rivers and streams swollen by rainstorms and spring melt, and powered by the full gravity of nearby mountains, rearrange outflowing channels of fresh water. Seasonally extreme tides and storms, pushed by the unrelenting force of the Pacific Ocean, alter the configuration of the estuarine shorelines. Landforms, such as barrier islands or peninsulas, provide shelter from the full force of ocean waves, winds, and storms.

121

Deemed one of the most productive ecological systems on earth, estuaries discreetly provide countless benefits to coastal and marine species, including people.

Most estuaries embrace wide intertidal flats of mud and sand, where the mouths of glacier-fed rivers and streams merge with the saline sea, creating hummocks of sedges incised with networks of drainage rivulets. Other estuaries, however, are located upstream and beyond the mouths of waterways in low lying islands and meadows surrounded by braids of brackish tidal streams.

Reflecting the transitional nature of estuaries, fluctuating dilutions of nutrient-rich fresh and salt water change daily and seasonally with rainfall, tides, evaporation, and distance from the mouths of rivers and streams. As a result, these estuarine waters are home to a diversity of life.

The open tidal spaces are meeting, feeding, mating, and playgrounds for terrestrial mammals and migratory birds (such as common mergansers, northern shovellers, Barrow's goldeneyes, American wigeons, mallards, occasionally tundra swans, sandhill cranes), as well as amphibians, gastropods, arthropods, and insects. Phytoplankton (diatoms, dinoflagellates) are abundant in the sediment, and a primary source of food for many organisms in estuaries, including bacteria, is detritus from the settlement of sedimentation and decomposing organisms.

Mud flats and murky shallows offer essential environments for fish, Dungeness crabs, oysters, and clams, while closer to the forest edge, Pacific crabapple and hawthorn, adorned with epiphytic plants, shelter rufous hummingbirds. Salmonberry and wild flowers abound: rice root lily, Douglas aster, kneeling angelica, silverweed, Indian paintbrush.

The flats are bathed twice daily by tides that deliver an assortment of organic refuse from the open seas—dead fish, birds, flotillas of jellyfish, and occasionally giant Humboldt squid, reclaimed by wolf pups as playthings. Washed up remains feed scavenging wolves that patrol the flats in perfect synchrony with the tides. In the early spring, lethargic black and grizzly bears search for highly nutritious herring eggs stranded by receding tides and forage on emerging green vegetation such as sedges and skunk cabbage. On the exposed beaches, buried clams spit and shorebirds peck at sandhoppers and shrimp. Glaucouswinged gulls float and screech. They forage on sea stars and spawning herring, staying alert to every edible opportunity.

Bald eagles and ravens survey the flats from their perches on nearby trees while seals sunbathe on rocks and exposed stumps. Tracks in the mud testify to the travels of animals, and scats chronicle the variety of the food supply. Black bears, grizzly bears, wolves, and Sitka deer flatten patches of sedges to rest in the morning sun. Sometimes a bloody, trampled space and some scant remains signify a successful hunt. The air is full of dragonflies and the muted sounds of insects and flapping wings. The smells are rich with decay and life, blurring the distinction between the two.

For many species, estuaries are transitional areas between fresh and salt water as well as between larval and adult stages. Even in winter estuaries are important areas for herring and migrating eulachons (oolichans). Larval eulachons use estuaries for their early life stage, with estuarine vegetation like sedge and eelgrass providing shelter from predators as well as opportunities to forage for food. Some marine species such as salmon spend most of their life in the open ocean but return to estuaries and connected rivers and streams to spawn. Tidal waters flush saline water back through narrow fiords, offering chemical cues for the salmon to migrate.

Salmon are the foundation of coastal ecology. During seasonal migrations to their natal estuaries and respective mating streams, five

five distinct species of salmon surrender tons of protein and nitrogen to the environment. Pink, chum, and coho salmon spawn in the continuous gravel beds that underlie the first several kilometres of the meandering rivers that feed the estuaries. Sockeye and Chinook travel further upstream to allow their smolts to rear in the deep lakes that feed the rivers. Forest growth over eons can be measured by the cycles of salmon abundance. Many species of birds, such as gulls, cranes, ducks, and perching birds, include salmon or their eggs in their seasonal diet, as do many mammals: mice; wolves; grizzly, black and spirit bears; river and sea otters; members of the weasel family such as short-tailed weasels, wolverines, mink, and martens. Their welfare depends on reliable salmon migrations.

Humans are also foragers of the rich foods found in estuaries. Coastal First Nations have long harvested sea asparagus, seaweed, shellfish, herring eggs strung on eelgrass, bulbs and roots, bird eggs, and eulachons. This tradition continues and includes some commercial harvesting.

Contemporary threats to estuaries are rising sea levels; acidification of ocean waters; amplified and protracted wake activity from marine traffic; increased sedimentation originating from industrial forestry (clearcuts, logging roads); and pollution in the form of terrestrial and marine contamination. Burgeoning human activities, the ominous pressures of climate change, and novel diseases are aggravating these threats, making estuaries a vital priority for research and preservation. The lesson is that to date, we have mistakenly and precariously assumed estuaries are resilient, when the safer assumption is of their fragility and vulnerability.

Deemed one of the most productive ecological systems on Earth, estuaries discreetly provide countless benefits to coastal and marine species, including people. Among these are the filtering of industrial, airborne, and agricultural pollutants, as well as the stabilization of

Nootka lupines | SHERRY KIRKVOLD

shorelines. Moreover, many recreational and economic activities, such as tourism and subsistence or commercial fishing, directly depend on estuarine health. Clearly, damaged and ecologically impoverished estuaries cannot sustain the wild species and people that depend on them, and the consequences have global implications.

123

DR. PAUL C. PAQUET has served as Raincoast's senior scientist for more than twelve years. He is an adjunct professor at the Universities of Calgary, Manitoba, and New Brunswick, and a faculty associate at Guelph University. An authority on mammalian carnivores, Paul has written many scientific articles and books. He recently co-authored *The World of Wolves: New Perspectives on Ecology, Behaviour and Management* and *A New Era for Wolves and People: Wolf Recovery, Human Attitudes, and Policy.*

ANITA ROCAMORA is an internationally acclaimed ceramist and sculptor whose award-winning works are inspired by the exquisite engineering of nature. A longtime friend of Raincoast, her volunteer work on behalf of nature and wildlife takes the form of writing, illustration, sculpture, scat collection, and occasional "bon mots."

It is a dream that the transcendentally beautiful northern coast of British Columbia could be saved from the kind of industrial practices that make a grotesque joke of phrases such as "job creation," "world-class safety standards," and "resource development." How can there be any justification for putting this extraordinary, productive world at risk?

The profound grief many of us feel witnessing the effects of an oil spill, or a clearcut that has destroyed a watershed, can only be borne by channelling that sadness and anger into the work of creating alternatives. My paintings reflect love of the complex, mysterious natural world and hope for the joy inherent in the lives of its creatures.

LISSA CALVERT

MERCEDES CALVERT

Thousands of Lissa Calvert's images grace Canadian and US homes in the form of original paintings, posters, art cards, and limited edition prints. Her original works are held in corporate and private collections in Canada and internationally.

Lissa, who has donated many paintings to environmental causes, currently lives and works in Sooke, BC, on a small river estuary rich with inspiration and close to the forest and ocean that sustain the heart of her work. Most of Lissa's landscapes are imaginary, and all the paintings start with a pencil sketch. If the painting is based on reality, with an animal in the composition, she uses a variety of reference materials for detail: photo libraries, her own reference photos, skulls, and field sketches.

>
Abundant Life
Acrylic on canvas
61 x 76 cm

Klemtu

RAY WARD

KAJ R. SVENSSON

Born in Comox, BC, and currently residing in Nanaimo, Ray spent a great deal of his youth drawing, painting, and being outdoors. A graduate of Capilano College's commercial art program, Ray changed his focus to fine art and has been displaying his work in galleries since 1998. His work can be found in private collections in Canada, the USA, Europe, Asia, and Australia and has been published in several magazines.

Vancouver Island never ceases to provide Ray with inspiration. The West Coast in particular has grabbed his attention, from the rugged beauty of its rocky shorelines and weather-worn trees, to the wide sandy bays and ever-changing tidal pools, to the calm coves and estuaries. "I enjoy the challenge of trying to capture the effects of fleeting light and atmosphere, such as the drama of a passing storm or the radiance of a winter sky moments before the sun sets."

>
Refuge
Oil on birch
61 x 76 cm

Ravens in Klemtu

TERRY ISAAC

KAJ R. SVENSSON

Internationally acclaimed wildlife artist Terry Isaac now lives in Penticton, BC. His love affair with nature provides the inspiration for his paintings—anything from a bird or flower in his own backyard to the captivating vistas of the west. A chance meeting with legendary wildlife artist Robert Bateman in the 1980s helped launch his professional career. Since then he has strived to capture "magical moments in nature" that appear with the right lighting, colour, and atmospheric conditions. He is inspired by large dramatic panoramas as well as close-up views of animal behaviour.

>
Mussel Inlet Grizzly
Acrylic on board
51 x 76 cm

D. F. GRAY

BEN FOX

Daniel Francis Gray, born in Vancouver in 1947, has worked in soft pastel since 1975. He lives in Errington on Vancouver Island, near the coast where he is most at home. He has been designated "Premier Pastellist of Canada" by the Pastel Society of Canada, and Steveston's Grand Prix of Art Trophy is named *The Gray Cup* for Dan's dedication to plein air.

Dan is the founder of the Grand Prix d'Art of Qualicum Beach, now in its twentieth year. Recently Dan represented Qualicum Beach at the 2010 Winter Olympics, and his work on a project to paint 2,010 people from life ended with more than 2,500 figures. In 2011 he curated a show of historical and contemporary Canadian pastels, *Pastel by Invite.*

>
Ancient Fishtrap,
Desbrisay Bay
Soft pastel on paper
61 x 46 cm

PEGGY SOWDEN

SHERRY KIRKVOLD

>
A Fragile Place
This Estuary
Acrylic on canvas
45 x 60 cm

Peggy's love of painting and wild places began as a child. Always encouraged by her mother—a landscape painter—to look, explore, and interpret what she saw, Peggy developed an early appreciation for the art process. Her father, an avid outdoorsman, took her family into the wilds of British Columbia, and from these summer adventures seeds were sown for a love of wilderness. Peggy studied visual arts in high school, worked as a naturalist, attended fine art school, worked as veterinarian, and painted the BC coast for many years; her two interests of art and nature are interwoven in a lifelong passion.

Creekwalker

On the Canoona River
I meet a man who walks this path each fall.
See how the river gives the Pink a hump,
he says,
the Chum a snout of snaggle teeth.

He opens a waterproof notebook.
Numbers must be fed:
how many fish have escaped
the mouth and the net.

The banks are littered with salmon
dragged from spawning beds,
eye sockets hollowed by ravens,
heads opened, brains licked out
by the bears' hot tongues.

He lives alone on a boat,
a creekwalker for thirty years.

We stand together in the rain
watching the water, no talk

of hunger, exhaustion,
death and birth. How a river
changes a man.

ALISON WATT

SALMON

The Great Provider

didn't always love salmon. I actually came by my obsession by default; salmon were simply the food supply for the finned, feathered, and furred creatures I was more enamoured with. My passion grew slowly. While blessed with exposure to many of the Central Coast's wild watersheds, it was an event in Rivers Inlet—a place of salmon and people, bears and rugged beauty, and ghosts and legends—that shifted my focus. The famed sockeye of Rivers Inlet imprinted on me in the fall of 1999, many years—decades even—after the demise of the great runs.

One hundred years earlier, the glacial rivers that flowed to Owikeno Lake at the head of the inlet teemed with salmon, primarily sockeye (*Oncorhynchus nerka*). The red dorsal humps, part of the physical transformation that male salmon undergo when competing for females, would break the water surface where the rivers shallow over the spawning gravels. The river dance of spawning salmon is a delicate trade-off between attracting mates and attracting bears. This dance, with its millions of annual participants from different species and races of salmon, was an event that occurred in virtually every freshwater river and stream accessible to Pacific salmon between 40° and 65° north latitude (California through British Columbia to Alaska) and

135

Top: Pink salmon | SHERRY KIRKVOLD
Centre, left to right:
Salmon stream | IVAN HUNTER
Spawned-out salmon | JAMEN RHODES
Below: Sockeye | SHERRY KIRKVOLD

The role of salmon in the greater ecosystem provides us with a lesson about connection, as salmon weave a thread that holds this coastal tapestry and its diverse inhabitants together.

east to the continental divide. Analysis of old cannery records indicates that upwards of 230 million salmon once returned to these watersheds, a quarter to a third of which spawned in BC.

While the importance of so many salmon to the diversity and productivity of coastal ecosystems has been elucidated since it first appeared in fisheries literature almost one hundred years ago, the underlying premise remains largely unchanged: large numbers of spawning salmon are important far beyond their role in reproduction.

Salmon carcasses—transferred from streams by hungry bears, wolves, eagles, and other predators and scavengers into the surrounding forest—provide a pulse of energy and nutrients to a radiating network of flora and fauna. In waves of consumption and decomposition, birds, mammals, small animals, insects, fungi, and bacteria consume and transform the bodies of salmon into mossy carpets, berry patches, towering cedars, spruce needles, feathers, fur, and even future generations of salmon themselves.

Amid the slow digestion and pungent dampness of an autumn temperate rainforest at the end of the salmon banquet, their fertilized eggs incubate in the frigid gravel of the riverbed. In the spring, tiny fry emerge from one of the five thousand spawning locations across the watersheds of Queen Charlotte Basin, with very low odds for survival. Most embryos do not even reach this stage. Less than 1 percent will likely reach adulthood and make the journey home to spawn.

For centuries, salmon have emerged from eggs, migrated thousands of kilometres, and returned to spawn and die on the same gravel beds from which they were born. This repeated use by generations of salmon has given rise to thousands of salmon populations adapted to specific sets of stream or local conditions. This fidelity has established 249 distinct races of salmon grouped according to their genes, behaviour, and lifestyle choices—just within the Queen Charlotte Basin. This also represents more than half of the diversity within all of Canada's Pacific salmon and accounts for the difficulty in restoring salmon to places where they no longer exist.

The preservation of local adaptations is one of the most important objectives of conservation. In the same way that a diverse investment portfolio enables stable financial returns under changing economic conditions, biological diversity creates the resilience to withstand natural cycles and persist under stress. The ability to survive changing conditions is part and parcel of being a salmon, but having the full evolutionary tool kit is critical to its success. A remarkable feature of salmon is that every generalization comes with an exception. The ability of Owikeno Lake in Rivers Inlet to produce the abundance of sockeye that supported fourteen canneries defies logic, or science anyway.

While the true historic abundance may never be known, three million sockeye once used the rivers and lake to rear their offspring. This is even more remarkable given that glacial lakes discourage light penetration. Without light and accompanying nutrients, food for young salmon is sparse. Despite this, the sockeye, four other species of salmon, some of the world's largest grizzly bears, and the Owikeno People lived with the bounty for generations.

Salmon carcass nourishes the forest | SHERRY KIRKVOLD

With the arrival of the canneries in the late 1800s everything changed, and quickly. They reigned and fell by 1960. In their heyday, 1,100 gillnets fished in the mouth of the inlet. The largest catch on record occurred in the late 1960s at 2.7 million sockeye. After that the abundance started to decline. In 1996 the fishery closed. In 1999 the unthinkable happened. In a story that almost rivals the passenger pigeon, 3,600 sockeye were counted returning to lake. The run had collapsed. As a consequence, the starving grizzly bears, whose fall salmon supply failed to materialize, wandered into the village looking for food; fourteen were shot along with two black bears. The ecosystem, because of lost salmon abundance, had its first documented victims.

There are valid reasons to believe that fishing alone did not cause the collapse, and the events and delicate timing needed for young salmon to migrate were mismatched by a series of local and broad changes to climate, habitat, and the stress that comes with low numbers. Regardless, it's a hard sell that human interference wasn't involved. Still today, the fishery remains closed.

Salmon and bears are sentinels of ecosystem health. When salmon are plentiful, grizzlies are bigger, more numerous, and have more cubs. Further, they can afford to high-grade, which benefits everyone. When bears select the rich fatty eggs and brain, the leftovers feed other animals and fertilize the streamside. This boosts the value of food for bears and transfers more nutrients and energy to other consumers. In contrast, when salmon are scarce, grizzlies produce fewer cubs—

if any—and eat more of each individual fish. Less discarded salmon then enters the surrounding ecosystem, with fewer benefits for other wildlife and ecosystem components.

The role of salmon in the greater ecosystem provides us with a lesson about connection, as salmon weave a thread that holds this coastal tapestry and its diverse inhabitants together.

MISTY MACDUFFEE is a biologist with Raincoast's Wild Salmon Program. She has spent the last fifteen years working in BC's coastal watersheds. To gain insight into the cause of the Rivers Inlet salmon collapse, she extracted sediment cores from the bottom of Owikeno Lake. Her work is motivated by a desire to change fisheries management so that all salmon-eaters—including bears, wolves, eagles, and whales—are considered when nets and hooks are placed on the routes of returning salmon.

Rivers Inlet has a unique Chinook salmon enhancement program. The Good Hope Cannery

has been promoting catch and release of these big fish for many years—a rare undertaking for

a commercial sport-fishing lodge. My participation in this program has been highly rewarding,

and I am grateful for the commitment to ensure these same experiences for future generations.

Rivers Inlet lies west of the proposed tanker route. This is just one of the priceless experiences

in jeopardy if we allow supertankers carrying diluted bitumen on this coast. The likelihood of a

spill is certain, and we cannot allow this to happen. We must keep ever vigilant of the threats to

our beautiful BC coast.

ROY HENRY VICKERS

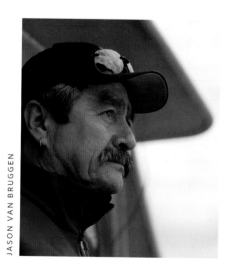

JASON VAN BRUGGEN

Canadian artist Roy Henry Vickers is a world-renowned printmaker, painter, carver, author, and designer whose signature style fuses the traditional images of his West Coast native ancestry with the realism of his British heritage. His artwork is held in museums and private collections across Canada and the world and is mostly sold through his artist owned and operated gallery in Tofino, British Columbia. In addition, Roy is a recognized leader in the First Nations community and is a tireless spokesperson for recovery from addictions and abuse. Roy's prolific career began after studying traditional Native art at the Gitanmaax School of Northwest Coast Indian Art in 'Ksan, British Columbia. Influenced by his mixed heritage, he developed a unique artistic style, which is immediately identifiable through its clean lines, vivid colours, and natural themes drawn from the rugged beauty of BC's West Coast.

>
Wonnok
Rivers Inlet
Serigraph print
47 x 69 cm

great contrast of rock and shadow

Old snag bleached out in sun causes excellent reflection

ESTHER SAMPLE

KAJ R. SVENSSON

Having grown up on the BC coast, Esther developed a passion for the sea and love for the shoreline. As an adult, she became a commercial fisherman for many years. The time she spent working on and travelling the span of the coast deepened her love for life on the water and shaped her artistic eye. With a growing family soon too large for the boat, she moved on from fishing, turning her focus to painting. Largely self-taught, Esther spent fifteen years using watercolours and pencil before settling into acrylics. It is here that she has found her niche in the brightly saturated medium.

In November 2011, Esther was the first woman to win the Pacific Salmon Foundation's Salmon Stamp award with the painting *Hunger Strikes*. She works from her home studio in Comox where she can easily draw inspiration from the beauty that surrounds her.

>
Tranquil River Bend
Acrylic on canvas
61 x 91 cm

MEGAN DULCIE DILL

KAJ R. SVENSSON

Megan Dulcie Dill is an emerging British Columbia artist recognized for her contemporary interpretations of the natural world. What distinguishes her art is a combination of visibly physical brushwork with flowing passages of transparent paint. Luminous shapes emerge and come alive in her paintings through texture, colour, and shifting lines.

A full-time painter, Megan incorporates her love for the natural world in her paintings. Now residing on the Sunshine Coast of British Columbia, she is a graduate of the Nova Scotia College of Art & Design. She is involved in various community arts initiatives while also enjoying hiking and spending time with her young family. She has participated in shows across Canada, and her work can be found in collections across North America.

> *Dance of the Rainforest*
Oil and encaustic on wood panel
91 x 107 cm

Everyone Waits for the Salmon in progress.
When the Enbridge pipeline no longer is routed
to Kitimat on the BC coast, the threat of an oil
spill will no longer exist. The glass oil spill can be
removed from the bowl, bringing life and renewal
through the yearly spawning of the salmon.

CHERYL SAMUEL

GAYE ADAMS

Through research, enthusiasm, and a lot of patience, Cheryl Samuel triggered the revival of the ancient ceremonial art of Ravenstail weaving in Alaska, British Columbia, and Haida Gwaii. She is author of *The Chilkat Dancing Blanket* and *The Raven's Tail,* the two definitive books on Northwest Coast weaving.

Since 1984 she has taught at the University of Alaska, where she helped to establish a certificate program in indigenous weaving. As an artist/ weaver she has represented Canada in the Commonwealth Games Arts Festivals in both Edinburgh and Auckland. In recent years she has turned her expertise in teaching and weaving to her other passions: celtic drawing and wood-turned sculptures. Her current works are mixed media, combining weaving with woodturning, glass, metal, and stone. *Everyone Waits for the Salmon* is a heart-wrenching cry to stop the inevitable destruction that a pipeline would bring to our coast.

>
*Everyone Waits
for the Salmon*
Garry oak, pewter,
glass
42 x 42 x 22 cm

At first glance, the coast of British Columbia appears to hold out against the violence of the open Pacific. Look again, more closely. The land and sea, it turns out, are intricately coupled. Each year the sea delivers a gleaming river, a reverse flow from ocean to watershed, with determined and delicate precision into spawning beds: salmon flesh moving generously into every part of the ecosystem, from grizzlies and wolves to maggots and even needles at the tops of spruce trees.

Coastal First Peoples still rely on salmon, just as their ancestors did when the fish kept them from starving through the winters and created long hours of ease in which they were first able to make their extraordinary and beautiful art.

ALISON WATT

KIM WATERMAN

Alison Watt is a visual artist and writer whose painting and writing are both informed by the natural world. Her work includes botanical watercolours as well as still lifes, landscapes, and abstracts in mixed media, plaster, acrylic, and oil. Alison has shown her work in group and solo shows in Vancouver and on Vancouver Island, and she teaches painting in her studio on Protection Island (Nanaimo, BC) and abroad (southern France).

In her twenties Alison worked as a seabird biologist in the Scott Islands, an experience she transformed into the award-winning book *The Last Island, a Naturalist's Sojourn on Triangle Island.* She has sailed BC's West Coast and worked as a naturalist along its length, from the Strait of Georgia to Johnstone Strait, the Great Bear Rainforest, the Kitlope Valley, and Haida Gwaii.

>
Sockeye
Acrylic on canvas
46 x 91 cm

Cartographies sans bornes: Maps without Borders BETH CARRUTHERS

The artist is a translator; one who has learned to pass into her own language the languages gathered from stones, from birds, from dreams, from the body, from the material world, from the invisible world…from love.—JEANETTE WINTERSON, *Art Objects*

THE NORTHERN BRITISH COLUMBIA COAST is home to the last significant temperate coastal rainforest on the planet—intact and rare ecosystem communities, some of which never experienced the glaciation of the last ice age. Those visitors who take the time to travel the West Coast are overwhelmed by the beauty and lush life to be found here.

There is no place elsewhere like this place, and even if there were, this would in no way decrease its value. Beyond scientific arguments, the value of home, of culture, and of community is not to be found in corporate ledgers or GDPs. Also not found there are these rich waters, deep forests, and myriad other creatures with whom we share this complex and astonishing coastal habitat—one that we require every bit as much as do these humpbacks, bears, wolves, and ravens. So rare a gem is this place that it is imperative that the rest of the world know and understand the value of its being, and that this being must be respected.

This precious bit of wild is important to everyone alive in this world, being the last place of its kind. As such, it is a matrix of life and meaning and a taproot into the depths of ourselves. The threat represented by dozens of VLCCs (very large crude carriers), each carrying some 227,000 dead weight tonnes of diluted bitumen through these wild and dangerous winding waterways, and the inevitable consequences of doing so, provides a terrifying vision.

Fear often causes us to disengage. One of the best responses to terrifying visions is the power of art. Art is not the first option most people consider for effective action, but recall for a moment that for centuries art and artists have been targeted for control or repression by dictators. If art were merely a nice bit of icing on the cultural cake, this would not be the case.

In her book *Art Objects,* writer Jeanette Winterson reminds us that artists deal in visions. And in many cultures, visions are recognized as messages from something or someone more than human, from beyond the boundaries of our standard perceptual map of the world.

In contradistinction to many campaigns on behalf of the wild, which offer us visions of broken lands and poisoned waters, the artworks in this book affirm the life of this place; they meet head-on the nightmare vision of oil-drenched sea and shore. These works, in their strength and beauty, open us, affirm what is here, and call for a different future for this place than that planned by corporate interest. These works speak on behalf of this place, of community, and they speak from the heart. They call us to stand forth ourselves and speak on behalf of this place.

An artwork is not simply a document, an image, or a replication. In the artwork, the perceptual presence and intention of the artist, and the voice and presence of the place itself, may be discerned. While a range of artistic styles and mediums is readily seen in this collection, the particular aspects of place that called each person to make this or that specific work are also revealed, and they too account for variation. For some artists the broad vistas and long views called; for others, it was the small, the close detail. But in all cases, these are intimate, relational works, and they invite the viewer into a world.

The wind-stirred feathers and steely eye of an eagle, the brilliant colours where sea meets shore, the secret worlds of sea stars and rockfish, the forever line of sight down a fiord, masks and bowls, the slap of a tail fluke, the flash of a wing, the feathery bowing of cedar, and the depth of green—each embodies the presence of place.

In his book *The Land Ethic*, Aldo Leopold (often called the father of environmentalism in North America) famously said, "We can be ethical in relation only with that which we can see, feel, understand, love, or otherwise have faith in." I have heard doctoral candidates open their dissertation defence citing love of place as the driving force behind their work. There is something potent and precious here that defies measurement or apprehension through the standards by which industrial culture measures meaning and value. Leopold spoke of ethics, of values, of their relationship to love. For those who live far from this place, it is this art that can open the door of perception so that anyone can, from afar, feel and experience the wonder and love of this place. Visions and artworks perform a subtle alchemy of transformation.

Uncontrollable, complex, and powerful, profound beauty troubles the waters of the usual and acceptable and stirs the depths. It opens the heart and the mind—and these works are beautiful.

Psychologist Piero Ferruci, in his book *Beauty and the Soul*, claims that when we experience beauty we are held "in a state of mindfulness that does not admit distraction or escape. We are here with our whole being. This is our *kairos*, as it was called in ancient Greece: the moment of opportunity, the timeless instant when revelation comes." And when it comes to bringing the world onside, to the protection of this place, we are in need of revelation.

These works welcome the world to this fecund green place of beauty and threat; to the last great northern rainforest; to the last clear shores of, as Terry Glavin named it, the last great sea. May we live up to its gifts, and may we love and care for it, for the sake of all our futures.

BETH CARRUTHERS is an internationally known writer, artist, educator, and curator. Focused on applied ethics and the vital role of aesthetic engagement in cultural change, her work addresses a range of topics within culture and sustainability. Recent and forthcoming publications include "Possible Worlds," a juror's essay in *The Time Is Now: Public Art of the Sustainable City,* and "A Subtle Activism of the Heart" in *Sustaining the West: Cultural Responses to Western Environments, Past and Present.*

Afterword

WADE DAVIS

ON THE COAST OF BRITISH COLUMBIA everything begins with wind and rain, the open expanse of the Pacific, and the steep escarpment of mountains that makes possible the constant cycling of water between land and sea. Autumn rains last until those of spring, and months pass without a sign of the sun. Sometimes the rain falls as mist, and moisture is raked from the air by the canopy of the forest. At other times, the storms are torrential and daily precipitation is measured in inches. The rains draw nutrients from the soil, carrying vital food into rivers and streams that fall away to the sea and support the greatest coastal marine diversity on Earth. In the estuaries and tidal flats, in shallows that merge with the wetlands, are more than six hundred types of seaweed and forty species of sea stars. Farther offshore, vast underwater kelp forests shelter hundreds of forms of life, which in turn support a food chain that reaches into the sky to nourish dozens of species of seabirds.

The land provides for life in the sea, but the sea in turn nurtures the land. Birds deposit excrement in the moss, yielding tonnes of nitrogen and phosphorous which are washed into the soil by winter rains. Salmon return by the millions to their natal streams, providing food for eagles and ravens, grizzly and black bears, killer whales, river otters, and more than twenty other mammals of sea and forest. Their journey complete, the sockeye and coho, Chinooks, chums, and pinks drift downstream in death and are slowly absorbed back into the nutrient cycle of life. In the end there is no separation between forest and ocean, between the creatures of the land and those of the sea. Every living thing on the raincoast ultimately responds to the same ecological rhythm. All are interdependent.

Living from nature, and lacking the technology to dominate it, the first people on the coast, the First Nations, watched the earth for signs. The flight of eagles helped fishermen track salmon. Sandhill cranes heralded the onset of herring runs. The flowering of certain plants brought families to the shore to gather clams, but if ravens and crows abandoned the beach, so did the people, for it was a sure indication that the shellfish were toxic. Between humans and animals there was a constant dialogue, expressed in physical action, in gesture and repartee, but also in myths and stories that resonated with magical and mystical ideas. The Tlingit addressed plants as spirits, offering prayers before harvesting a tree. Nuu-chah-nulth ceremonies sought protection for the hunter and beseeched whales to give freely of their lives. When raging currents threatened Haida war parties, the paddlers scattered swan feathers upon the water to calm the sea. Encounters with grizzly bears brought power to the Gitxsan. The Kwakwaka'wakw dispatched initiates into the forest to seek Huxwhukw and the Crooked-Beak of Heaven, cannibal spirits living at the north end of the world.

For all of these cultures the land was alive—a dynamic force to be embraced and transformed by the human imagination. Mountains, rivers, and forests were not perceived as inanimate, as mere props on a stage upon which the human drama unfolds. There was a dialogue with the natural world as well as clear reciprocal expectations, for even as the Earth provided its bounty, so human beings were responsible for the well-being of the Earth. Whether this was true in some absolute sense is not the point. The significance lies in the manner in which the conviction played out in the day-to-day lives of the people. A child raised to revere the forest as the domain of the spirits will be a fundamentally different person from a child brought up to believe that a forest exists to be cut.

The artists celebrated in this stunning book express their love of the coast in many mediums and in their own idiosyncratic styles. But what draws their passions into a single dazzling vision is a common conviction that we must fundamentally change the way we interact with the natural world. The First Nations thrived on the Pacific Coast for centuries, leaving in their wake the lightest of ecological footprints. Modern industrial society, by contrast, has in but three generations torn these forests asunder. Along the coast and throughout the northern interior—from the islands of Haida Gwaii to the Sacred Headwaters of the Tahltan—the provincial authorities continue to endorse economic policies that imply the violation of our natural capital on a massive scale. In a country of immense capacity, whose people are among the most highly educated and sophisticated to be found in any nation, the government continues to suggest that the primary way of generating economic prosperity must remain the exploitation of our forests, mountains, and rivers on an industrial scale. This surely indicates less a dearth of economic options than a lack of imagination on the part of those we elect to office.

Those who have come together to offer their work and artistic spirit to this book are saying that there is another way, another vision of life on the coast of British Columbia. For a century we have sacrificed the salmon and the rivers, the forests and mountains on the altar of our prosperity. Surely it is time to shatter this way of thinking and recognize that the well-being of these salmon forests is our prosperity. It is this vision that turns their work into a single force, a call for the protection of the land, and a prayer for the well-being of all, including the countless generations still waiting to be born.

WADE DAVIS is an explorer-in-residence at the National Geographic Society and the author of seventeen books including *One River, The Wayfinders, The Sacred Headwaters, Into the Silence*, and *River Notes*. His many film credits include *Light at the Edge of the World*, an eight-hour documentary series written and produced for National Geographic. In 2009 he received the Gold Medal from the Royal Canadian Geographical Society for his contributions to anthropology and conservation. He is also the 2011 recipient of the Explorers Medal, the highest award of the Explorers Club, and the 2012 David Fairchild Medal for Plant Exploration.

Investigate. Inform. Inspire.

CHRIS GENOVALI

THE RAINCOAST CONSERVATION FOUNDATION is a team of conservationists and scientists empowered by our research to protect the lands, waters, and wildlife of coastal British Columbia. Our presence on the ground and water provides us with a deep-rooted understanding of this vast coastline. Raincoast works in the traditional territories of coastal First Nations. We value our partnerships with these nations and believe we achieve more working together than independently.

Raincoast's mandate is to *investigate, inform,* and *inspire.* Using the best science, we investigate to understand coastal species and ecology. We inform by bringing science to decision makers and communities. We inspire people to be ambassadors for, and protectors of, this priceless coast. We brand this *informed advocacy*: a unique blend of rigorous science, applied ethics, and grassroots activism.

We regard coastal BC's majestic diversity of plants and animals as assets to nurture rather than resources to exploit. Over the past decade Raincoast has worked tirelessly to conserve eco-culturally significant areas of the BC coast. Our vision is to safeguard the lives and protect the habitats of wide-ranging animals like grizzly bears and wolves, whose life requisites include those of many other species. Protecting these iconic species and their environments extends an umbrella of protection for the many other plants and animals that make up the larger ecological community. We believe this approach will help ensure all species, including people, can thrive.

Our applied conservation science is about discovery, practical insights, and solutions. Raincoast's work falls into three streams: our *Oil-Free Coast* initiative focuses on the threats posed to the BC coast from the creation of an energy corridor for tanker shipments of tar sands oil; our *Salmon For Wildlife* initiative assesses how salmon declines affect top-level terrestrial and marine predators and advocates for a sufficient food supply for bears, killer whales, and other species that depend on salmon; and our *Large Carnivore Conservation* initiative aims to protect apex and summit predators (such as wolves and grizzlies) by protecting food supply and habitat, attaining trophy hunting closures, and advocating for a wildlife welfare ethic.

Much of Raincoast's work is carried out on the S.V. *Achiever,* our Transport Canada-certified, 21-metre steel-hulled sloop. *Achiever* has been instrumental in Raincoast's science, education, and advocacy efforts over the years. Whether it is conducting gruelling line transect surveys through the Queen Charlotte Basin and Hecate Strait, supporting youth Rediscovery initiatives, or monitoring remote coastal watersheds, *Achiever* makes it possible for us to deliver on our mission and mandate.

Combining our research with education, our outreach in schools and communities mentors young leaders in science literacy, building their knowledge of, and passion for, our coastal environment. Embodying this approach, our Hakai-Raincoast Conservation Scholar

152

PHOTO: IAN JANSMA

initiative brings the University of Victoria into our applied science and academic pursuits.

Raincoast's publications in some of the world's most respected and influential scientific journals have attracted international media attention. We have been featured in television documentaries by National Geographic, Discovery Channel, CBC, and PBS; in natural history magazines such as the *Smithsonian, BBC Wildlife, Scientific American,* and *Canadian Geographic*; and in media coverage from CNN, NPR, BBC, *New York Times, The Guardian, Los Angeles Times, The Globe and Mail,* and more.

Raincoast is a lean organization, relying on the efforts of passionate students, volunteers, and a small dedicated staff. Tax-deductible charitable donations enable this special team to make a real difference on this coast.

CHRIS GENOVALI has served as executive director of Raincoast Conservation Foundation for fifteen years. His articles on wildlife and conservation issues have appeared in numerous publications, including the *Vancouver Sun, Victoria Times Colonist, The Ecologist, Seattle Post-Intelligencer, Edmonton Journal,* and *The Huffington Post.* He has also appeared as a spokesperson on radio and television outlets such as CBC's *As It Happens* and *Newsworld,* National Public Radio, Global TV, BBC Radio, and Knowledge Network.

Raincoast Conservation Foundation
PO Box 2429
Sidney, British Columbia V8L 3Y3
Canada

250.655.1229
www.raincoast.org

Message in a bottle

As part of an effort to understand ocean currents and how they would influence the movement of a potential oil spill, the Institute of Ocean Sciences, the Gitga'at First Nation, and Raincoast teamed up to drop five hundred "drift" bottles into the Pacific Ocean off Gil Island. Our trip to Hartley Bay on Achiever *had been auspicious, with brilliant sunny skies and an elephant seal sighting—a harbinger of good things to come. Successive pods of Pacific white-sided dolphins and Dall's porpoises enthusiastically escorted us, bow riding in the sparkling waves. School children from Hartley Bay dropped the glass bottles from* Achiever *into Wright Sound the following day, each containing labels and contact instructions. The day of the drop was absolute magic, as we counted twenty humpback whales breaching at various intervals. Humpback recovery in the region could be put in jeopardy by a catastrophic oil spill.*

The bottle drop completed, Achiever *continued to sit stationary with the engine off. Two large humpbacks approached the boat and for a full hour put on an amazing show. The whales frolicked around and underneath the boat displaying their tail flukes, lobtailing, blowing at the surface, showering us with their misty breath, and repeatedly spyhopping so close we were literally eye to eye.*

The synchronicity of the bottle drop, carried out by Hartley Bay's youth, and the humpbacks' subsequent display was not lost on us. In fact, the symbolism sent shivers up our spines. Here were two groups— one whale, one human—both vulnerable to any potential oil spill on this coast and both seeming to salute one another in the goal of preserving our unspoiled waters.—C.G.

153

Artists working on the deck of Raincoast's research vessel *Achiever*. PHOTO | BEN FOX

ACKNOWLEDGEMENTS

There are times when you feel you must take action. The threat of a catastrophic oil spill resulting from oil supertankers plying the waters of the Central and North Coast of BC is one of those times. Our goal is to show some of what is at stake—the magnificent, beautiful, fully functioning ecosystems of Canada's Raincoast.

In 1989 Mark Hobson brought one hundred artists together to collaborate with the Western Wilderness Committee on the book *Carmanah, Artisic Visions of an Ancient Rainforest*. Public pressure led to the end of logging and the creation of a new provincial park in that area. In November 2011, Mark began to think that a similar project could be undertaken on the Central Coast, but getting artists to the Great Bear Rainforest is exponentially more difficult than to Carmanah.

Brian Falconer, with thirty-five years of experience as a captain on the coast, was one of the first collaborators. Brian, as the marine operations coordinator for the Raincoast Conservation Foundation, took little time to bring that organization on board.

A core group of volunteers met in December 2011 and set a goal of arranging for fifty artists to visit the Great Bear Rainforest in June 2012, to complete a book and film of the project by November 2012, and to set up a series of travelling art shows.

Chris Genovali and Misty MacDuffee from Raincoast, both with sixteen years of dedication, conservation advocacy and scientific research in the area, took on fundraising for the project and assisted with its organization. They also arranged to have the Raincoast scientists and others write the chapters. Brian's numerous connections and friendships, especially with First Nation communities, were invaluable as he coordinated the complex logistics for the artists' expeditions.

Mark Hobson assumed the role of overall project manager as well as looking after the communications with the artists. Mark also participated as an artist and photographer.

Sherry Kirkvold, a naturalist by profession who was also involved with *Carmanah*, undertook editing the book and assembling the texts. She also contributed photographs from her work on the coast. Amy Reiswig, a senior editor for Hansard at the Legislative Assembly of BC and writer for *Focus* magazine, came on board as Associate Editor to lend her skills in crafting the words. Thora O'Grady assisted with proofing the final manuscript.

Frances Hunter, from Beacon Hill Communications, took on the task of book design and coordinating all the materials required from the artists. Her vision also included poetry, and she initiated a process to select poems for each chapter.

Ernst Vegt, from Coast Imaging Arts, contributed expertise in colour optimizing and proofing all the images in the book. Eckhard Zeidler, Z-Point Graphics, created the panoramic map.

Susan McIntyre acted as the media coordinator, and Barbara Thomas joined the team to produce an e-book version of the project.

Jeff Whiting, with his background as the president and founder of the Artists for Conservation Foundation, provided advice on gathering and choosing the artists. Craig Benson was one of the first artists to come on board and participated in the organizational meetings as well as being our spokesperson at the project launch.

With a very tight timetable, the selection of artists was by invitation. We believed it was very important to include artists from the areas near the proposed pipeline and tanker routes, and we recognize there were many others who would have liked to participate.

The problem of where to put fifty artists in a vast wilderness was quickly resolved. Each of the lodges and tour boat operators contacted agreed to host groups of artists. We have included information on each operation, but in particular we would like to thank Christina Munck and Eric Peterson at Hakai Institute, Tim McGrady and Doug Neasloss of Spirit Bear Lodge, and Michael Uehara of King Pacific Lodge as well as the boat operators, Ross Campbell and Fern Kornelsen of the *Columbia III*, Kevin Smith and Maureen Gordon of the *Maple Leaf*, and Raincoast Conservation with their research vessel *Achiever*. We would also like to thank all those who crewed on those boats and worked in the lodges. Marven Robinson provided artist transportation out of Hartley Bay, Juergen Puetter provided air transport for artists and media, and Randy Burke also offered space on the *Island Roamer*.

Accompanying the artist expeditions were filmmakers and photographers. Cameron Dennison of StrongHeart Productions, who took on the overall production of a film, *Reflections: Art for an Oil-Free Coast*, was accompanied by Robin Hood, Ben Fox, and Kimberly Johnston. Kaj Svensson, Ben Fox, Mark Hobson, and Sherry Kirkvold also travelled with the artists to provide still photography.

There are many other contributors we would like to acknowledge, and many are credited in the book or can be found in the contributors pages. There are the many photographers who either photographed the artworks and the artists or provided images for the chapters. We also thank the poets, the writers, and the artists.

We especially thank all who supported the fundraising efforts by donating funds or services.

As the project moves forward, there are those who are helping to frame the art and organize the art shows, and while we can't list everyone by name at press time, know that we thank each of you for your contribution. Many people came together to support this project. Together we hope that by raising awareness, we can keep this an oil-free coast.

156

CONTRIBUTORS

VISUAL ARTISTS

Gaye Adams
www.gayeadams.com

Harold Allanson
www.haroldallanson.ca

Shawn Aster
shawnaster@hotmail.com

Carol Young Bagshaw
www.carolyoung.ca

Robert Bateman
www.robertbateman.ca

Craig Benson
www.craigarthurbenson.com

Dianne Bersea
www.islemuse.com/
diannber1.html

Lissa Calvert
www.lissacalvert.ca

Carl Chaplin
www.CarlChaplin.ca

Brent Cooke
www.castartstudio.com

Ben Davidson
www.allaboutuarts.ca

Robert Davidson
www.robertdavidson.ca

Megan Dulcie Dill
www.mdill.com

Collin Elder
www.collinelder.com

Carol Evans
www.carolevans.com

Linda Dayan Frimer
www.lindafrimer.ca

David Goatley
www.davidgoatley.com

D.F. Gray
www.dfgray.com

Kindrie Grove
www.kindriegrove.com

W. Allan Hancock
www.wallanhancock.com

Julia Hargreaves
www.juliahargreaves.com

Bill Helin
www.billhelin.com

Linda Heslop
www.fullcirclestudio.ca

Mark Hobson
www.markhobson.com

Terry Isaac
www.terryisaacsart.com

Kevin Johnson
www.artguykevin.com

Paul Jorgensen
jorg1@telus.net

Sheila E. Karrow
www.sheilakarrow.com

Stewart Marshall
250.973.2310

David McEown
www.artistjourneys.com

Dominik J. Modlinski
www.paintingjourneys.com

Mae Moore
www.maemoore.com

Dorset Norwich-Young
www.dorsetnorwichyoung.com

Michael O'Toole
www.whiterockgallery.com/
Michael_OToole.htm

Murray E. Phillips
www.murrayphillipsart.com

Ian Reid
nusi.reid@gmail.com

Janice Roberston
www.janicerobertson.ca

Esther Sample
www.esthersample.com

Cheryl Samuel
www.ravenstail.com

Peggy Sowden
davetpeggys@msn.com

Todd Stephens
todd.stephens@hotmail.com

Roberta Sutherland
www.robertapyxsutherland.com

Mike Svob
www.mikesvob.com

Chili Thom
www.chilithom.com

Roy Henry Vickers
www.royhenryvickers.com

Ray Ward
www.rayward.ca

Alison Watt
www.alisonwatt.ca

April White
www.aprilwhite.com

Jeffrey Gordon Whiting
www.jeffreywhiting.com

Alan Wylie
www.alan-wylie.ca

PHOTOGRAPHERS

Gaye Adams

Scott August, 129

John Bagshaw, 69
www.johnbagshaw.com

Colin Bates

A. Michael Bezener, 89

Charles Brandt

Lorne Brownsey

Mercedes Calvert

Mark Carwardine
www.markcarwardine.com

Ted Clarke, 113
www.imagethisphoto.ca

Perry Danforth, 103

Chris Darimont

Nathan De Bruyn

Rob Destrubé, 25, 65, 71, 125, 145
www.destrube.com

Janet Dwyer, 49, 97
www.janetdwyer.com

Jonathan Dy
www.jonathandy.com

Ben Fox
www.benfox.ca

Daisy Gilardini, 63

Dirk Heydemann, 127

Sue Melto Helin

Mark Hobson

Ivan Hunter
www.ivanhunter.com

Tim Irwin

Ian Jansma

Mark Kaarremaa, 147

Bryn King

Sherry Kirkvold

Jack Litrell

Ron Ling, cover, 43, 83, 95, 111
www.zheeclay.com

Kerri Malone

Guillaume Mazille

Ken Nagai, 109

Marie O'Shaughnessy

Murray Phillips

Klaus Pommerenke
www.bears-and-more.de

Tom Reimchen

Jamen Rhodes
www.jamenrhodes.com

Eric Sambol
www.ericsambol.com

Jason Shafto
www.fullmoonphoto.ca

Eric James Soltys, 87
www.spiritwrestler.com

Dane Stabel

Vivian Stephens

Francis Sullivan, 39, 119
www.francissullivanphoto.com

Kaj R. Svensson, 55, 73, 83, 133
www.kajrsvensson.com

Richard Trueman, 115
www.richardtrueman.com

Jason van Bruggen
www.jasonvanbruggen.com

Ernst Vegt, 23, 27, 29, 35, 37, 41, 51,
57, 81, 131
www.coastimagingarts.com

Kim Waterman

Mike Yip
www.vancouverislandbirds.com

POETS

YVONNE BLOMER is the artistic director of Planet Earth Poetry. Her first book, *a broken mirror, fallen leaf,* was shortlisted for the Gerald Lampert Memorial Award. Her most recent books include *Bicycle Brand Journey* with JackPine Press and *The Book of Places* with Black Moss Press.

KIM GOLDBERG is an award-winning poet and journalist living in Nanaimo, BC. She is the author of six books including *Red Zone* and *Where to See Wildlife on Vancouver Island.* She holds a degree in biology and is an avid birdwatcher, trailbreaker, and nature lover.

J. IRIBARNE lives on Vancouver Island in Canada where she teaches at Camosun College. She has published in *Arc, subTerrain, Room,* and other magazines, as well as co-authored *Climate Change: A Profile for Community Action.*

CHRISTINE LOWTHER is the author of *Half-Blood Poems, My Nature,* and *New Power* and is co-editor and co-author of *Writing the West Coast: In Love With Place.* Her work has appeared as Poetry-in-Transit and in literary journals and anthologies. She lives in Clayoquot Sound.

GARRY THOMAS MORSE has had two books of poetry published by LINEbooks, *Transversals for Orpheus* (2006) and *Streams* (2007); one collection of fiction published by Talonbooks, *Death in Vancouver* (2009); and two books of poetry published by Talonbooks, *After Jack* (2010) and *Discovery Passages* (2011)—the latter a finalist for the Governor General's Award for Poetry and for the Dorothy Livesay Poetry Prize. *Minor Episodes/ Major Ruckus* will be available from Talonbooks, Fall 2012.

STEVE NOYES has published seven books of fiction and poetry. *Rainbow Stage/Manchuria* is forthcoming with Oolichan Books. He has lived three of the past ten years in China. Today he lives in Victoria where he writes and works for the BC Ministry of Health.

PATRICK M. PILARSKI is the co-editor of *DailyHaiku* and poetry editor for *DailyHaiga.* His first full-length collection of poetry, *Huge Blue,* was published by Leaf Press in 2009, and he is the author of two short collections. Patrick has served as vice-president of the League of Canadian Poets and is a postdoctoral fellow in computing science at the University of Alberta.

EDEN ROBINSON is the author of *Traplines, Monkey Beach,* and *Blood Sports. Traplines* was a *New York Times* Notable Book of the Year and won Britain's Winifred Holtby Memorial Prize. *Monkey Beach* was nominated for the Giller Prize and the 2000 Governor General's Award for Fiction. Born in Kitamaat, Robinson is a member of the Haisla and Heiltsuk First Nations.

ALISON WATT is a painter and poet who lives on Protection Island, BC. Originally a biologist, she has published *The Last Island: a Naturalist's Sojourn on Triangle Island* (2003, winner of the Edna Staebler Award for non-fiction) and *Circadia* (2005, poetry).

157

HAKAI INSTITUTE

Calvert Island, BC
Box 309, Heriot Bay
BC V0P 1H0
Eric Peterson: eric@hakai.org
Christina Munck: christina@hakai.org
www.hakai.org

Hakai
Hakai Institute

Hakai Institute is a research, teaching, and meeting place located on an isolated island on the BC Central Coast. Research focuses on long-term monitoring of changes in the marine and terrestrial ecosystems around their base, and they also study evidence of the changes that have taken place during the 15,000 years since the end of the last Ice Age. This research touches upon marine and terrestrial ecology, earth sciences, and archaeology. Research is conducted by their staff and supplemented by partnerships with BC universities. The teaching program roughly matches the scope of their research, and it includes everything from formal courses offered by universities to short courses and workshops for First Nations resource managers and others with a direct stake in the Central Coast. The community programs focus mainly on Central Coast schools, and they emphasize science, outdoor recreation, and other activities for which Hakai is particularly well suited.

KING PACIFIC LODGE

Barnard Harbour, Princess Royal Island, BC
255 West 1st Street, Suite 214,
North Vancouver, BC V7M 3G8
1.888.592.5464 or 604.987.5452
info@kingpacificlodge.com
www.kingpacificlodge.com

King Pacific Lodge is a luxurious floating wilderness eco-resort located in the pristine Great Bear Rainforest on the North Coast of British Columbia. King Pacific Lodge offers world-class accommodations, unparalleled wilderness adventures, spectacular fishing, soothing spa experiences, and sensational culinary masterpieces. Whether you are hooking a 20 kilogram Chinook salmon, exploring the rugged coastline or sheltered bays by kayak, hiking to beautiful waterfalls,

searching for the rare and elusive Kermode (spirit) bear, or relaxing at the Rainforest Spa, King Pacific Lodge has something for everyone. Among its many accolades, King Pacific Lodge was selected as the Best Resort in Canada by Condé Nast Readers' Choice Awards in 2008, 2009, 2010, and 2011. It was also recognized as North America's Leading Green Hotel at the 2010, 2011 and 2012 World Travel Awards and was the recipient of the Travel & Leisure 2011 Global Vision Award for Sustainability.

SPIRIT BEAR LODGE

Klemtu, BC
Tim McGrady, General Manager
250.339.5644
explore@spiritbear.com
www.spiritbear.com

The modern waterfront Spirit Bear Lodge pays homage to the traditional houses built for thousands of years by West Coast First Nations. Spirit Bear Lodge offers multi-day bear viewing tour packages, which give guests the opportunity to experience the rich cultural and natural history of BC's wild coast. Tours include exploring the ancestral lands and traditional territory of the Kitasoo/Xai'xais First Nation, encompassing the natural habitat of the spirit bear in the Kitasoo Spirit Bear Conservancy.

MOTHERSHIP ADVENTURES

Mothership Adventures Inc.
Box 30, Heriot Bay, BC V0P 1H0
1.888.833.8887 or 1.250.202.3229
info@mothershipadventures.com
www.mothershipadventures.com

Mothership Adventures has been sea kayaking and cruising extensively on the British Columbia coast since 1995, aboard the 21-metre heritage vessel *Columbia III*. Built in 1956 for the Columbia Coast Mission, the *Columbia III* operated tirelessly for many years as a hospital ship serving the isolated communities and logging camps on BC's wild, remote shores. Now luxuriously refurbished and run as a small family business, the *Columbia III* and her professional crew bring visitors to explore the largest remaining temperate rainforest in the world.

Mothership Adventures is passionate about sharing their love and knowledge of this unique and beautiful place with guests from around the world, while also raising awareness of its need for protection. They feel extremely fortunate to live and work in one of the most diverse marine habitats on this planet. Their paddling and cruising season focuses on the orcas, white-sided dolphins, and humpback whales in the Broughton Archipelago and on the sea otters, grizzlies, spirit bears, and wolves in the Great Bear Rainforest.

"We feel an urgency to defend those who can't speak for themselves and are thrilled to be involved in the *Canada's Raincoast at Risk* art book project— our small contribution to an issue close to the hearts of many Canadians."

MAPLE LEAF ADVENTURES

Victoria, BC V8W 3Z1
1.888.599.5323 or +1-250.386.7245
info@MapleLeafAdventures.com
www.MapleLeafAdventures.com

Rated one of "Canada's Best Travel Experiences" by Frommer's, Maple Leaf Adventures has operated multi-day adventure cruises in BC since 1986, featuring spectacular wilderness, wildlife (whales, grizzly and spirit bears, seabirds, and more), and authentic BC culture. Travelling aboard a classic 28-metre BC sailing ship, the eight guests receive a high-quality, personalized adventure. Itineraries include Great Bear Rainforest, Haida Gwaii, Vancouver Island, Gulf Islands, and Alaska. In fact, their Great Bear Rainforest trip was recognized as part of *National Geographic Traveler*'s "50 Tours of a Lifetime." Trips benefit from expert guides, naturalists, and chefs, and from Maple Leaf's longstanding relationships with scientists and First Nations. Guests and guides go ashore often to explore rainforest, beaches, key wildlife viewing sites, and to visit villages. Guests are independent travelers—solo, couples, and extended families. Art and photography trips are also offered. Maple Leaf Adventures was honoured to host artists for the oil-free coast project. "This beautiful coast is the lifeblood of our company. It is part of our ethic to give back to conservation and our coastal community."

S.V. *ACHIEVER*

Raincoast Conservation Foundation
Box 2429, Sidney, BC V8L 3Y3
Brian Falconer: brian@raincoast.org
www.raincoast.org/about-raincoast/research-vessel/

One of the challenges of trying to do research on British Columbia's North and Central Coast is getting around. In 2003, Raincoast Conservation Foundation made an investment in *Achiever*, a 21-metre, steel-hulled sloop. She underwent an extensive refit—led by Raincoast's Brian Falconer, who also serves as her captain—being redesigned for capacity and versatility, as well as for certification by Transport Canada. Utilizing this sturdy, safe, and smartly designed working boat as their research platform, Raincoast undertakes science initiatives on its own and in partnership with other organizations, such as the Institute of Ocean Sciences and Simon Fraser University. *Achiever* is also chartered to academic institutions and government agencies conducting their own coastal research as well as to documentary film crews for media outlets such as NHK (Japan), BBC, and National Geographic.

BLUEWATER ADVENTURES

3-252 E First Street
North Vancouver, BC V7L 1B3
1.888.877.1770, 604.980.3800
explore@bluewateradventures.ca
www.bluewateradventures.ca

Since 1974, Bluewater Adventures' reputation has brought respected groups and people from around the world to enjoy "once-in-a-lifetime" wildlife and coastal First Nations cultural experiences. Multi-day, live-aboard trips explore the remote wilderness of coastal British Columbia and Southeast Alaska. Aboard the 21-metre expedition yachts, guests and crew keep watch for whales and other marine mammals, coastal birds, bears, old-growth forests, and ancient native villages. Experienced biologists, renowned resource people, and professional crew engage guests on these unique learning journeys. Trips specialize in wildlife behaviour, coastal ecology, and local history of the West Coast. A small group size of twelve to sixteen guests ensures quality, informality, and a "hands-on" experience for all aboard. Bluewater Adventures trips adhere to the principles of ecotourism: support local communities, promote conservation, ensure practices are low impact, and provide guests with world-class knowledge about the coast, wildlife, and First Nations' cultures.

Library and Archives Canada Cataloguing in Publication
Canada's raincoast at risk : art for an oil-free coast / foreword
    by David Suzuki ; afterword by Wade Davis.

ISBN 978-0-9688432-7-7

    1. Pacific Coast (B.C.)—Pictorial works. 2. Pacific Coast (B.C.)—
Literary collections. 3. Coastal ecology—British Columbia—Pacific Coast—
Pictorial works. 4. Coastal ecology—British Columbia—Pacific Coast—
Literary collections. I. Raincoast Conservation Foundation

FC3845.P2C36 2012   971.1'100222   C2012-905934-X

Editor: Sherry Kirkvold
Associate editor: Amy Reiswig
Art coordination: Mark Hobson
Design: Frances Hunter, Beacon Hill Communications Group
Colour separations, colour optimization: Ernst Vegt, Coast Imaging Arts
Map: Eckhard Zeidler
Title page photo: Sherry Kirkvold

Typefaces: FF Tundra, Font Shop International www.fontfont.com
Whitney, www.typography.com

Printed in Canada by Friesens, Altona, Manitoba

FSC
www.fsc.org
MIX
Paper from
responsible sources
FSC® C016245

Raincoast Conservation Foundation
PO Box 2429
Sidney, BC V8L 3Y3
250.655.1229

www.raincoast.org